Multiculturalism

Current Titles

Concepts in the Social Sciences

Multiculturalism

C. W. Watson

Open University Press
Buckingham · Philadelphia

Open University Press
Celtic Court
22 Ballmoor
Buckingham
MK18 1XW

email: enquiries@openup.co.uk
world wide web: www.openup.co.uk

and
325 Chestnut Street
Philadelphia, PA 19106, USA

First Published 2000

A catalogue record of this book is available from the British Library

ISBN 0 335 20520 8 (pb)   0 335 205216 0 (hb)

Library of Congress Cataloging-in-Publication Data available

Typeset by Type Study, Scarborough
Printed in Great Britain by St Edmundsbury Press, Bury St Edmunds

For Martina
Salah sesuatu untuk mengganti kursi

and for Geoffrey and Benedict, Dewi and Puteri
Anak istimewa yang senantiasa menggairahkan
kehidupan kami

Contents

Acknowledgements

I must thank various friends, colleagues and students for help with this book. First a word of collective thanks to my colleagues in the Department of Anthropology who agreed to let me have a lighter than normal teaching load for a term while I completed the manuscript. Thanks to John Clammer for some references to Chinese material; and to Bob Parkin for information on India. Two graduate students in our department also provided me with useful references, Alejandro Agudo-Sanchiz to Latin American material and Katharina Albert to recent writing on Germany.

A special word of thanks is due to Professor Ralph Grillo who looked over the whole manuscript carefully, made some astute comments and offered some excellent suggestions. Because I have not always followed his advice, it is especially important that I absolve him from responsibility for any of the book's shortcomings. For the latter I alone must take the blame.

And thanks once again to my family for tolerating my absence on the occasions when we should have been doing things together. *Terima kasih atas kesabaran.*

Introduction

The current voguishness of the term 'multiculturalism' and the frequency of its use not only in academic but also in popular writing should be enough to alert us to the likelihood that the word has come to mean different things to different people. To avoid the risk of ambiguity, we need to establish something of this range before taking the discussion further. (For an authoritative account of the recent origins of the term and an excellent introductory statement of the issues, see Wieviorka 1998.) One of the earliest modern uses of the term derives from the adjective 'multicultural', in particular as used in the phrases 'multicultural curriculum', 'multicultural education' and 'multicultural society'. The last term appears to give rise to the first two. What it denotes is a society in which there exist several cultures. The question of what precisely constitutes a culture is generally begged in this usage – though, if pressed, those who use the phrase would probably speak of cultures as referring to a common language, a shared history, a shared set of religious beliefs and moral values, and a shared geographical origin, all of which taken together define a sense of belonging to a specific group. It is not very satisfactory as a definition, and one might be hard put to defend all the criterial features of it, or to decide in difficult cases what was or was not a culture, but these ideas are the ones which people have in mind when they use the phrase 'multicultural society'. There is a notion of the distinctiveness of each culture, each separate from others, a notion which is vigorously challenged by modern anthropology which has emphasized time and time again the lack of any substantive boundary between cultures, but one which is for the moment entrenched in contemporary debates. To speak of a multicultural society, then, is to speak of a society – a state, a nation, a country, a region or even simply a bounded geo-graphical location such as a town or a school – composed of people who belong to different cultures.

Note, however, that there are other terms which can and have been used to describe the same phenomenon. For example, it was common in the social sciences before the rise of the word 'multi-cultural' to see reference to plural societies, and in common par-lance references are still frequently made to some of the large cities of the North (the northern hemisphere) as cosmopolitan – that is, containing citizens who have come from all four corners of the globe and settled there.[1] There are also at present frequent refer-ences to 'multiethnic societies', though, perhaps because that word is recognized to be a bastard conflation of words deriving from Latin and Greek, the preference is to use 'multiracial' or 'polyeth-nic' – much more the latter than the former because of the difficulty we now have with the word 'race' which has spurious biological connotations and is better avoided. 'Polyethnic' seems at least for the moment a much more acceptable word, with its suggestion of a self-constructed definition of belonging to a specific cultural (ethnic) group; nevertheless its use is largely confined to discussion in academic circles and 'multicultural' is still the preferred word.

The reason for the continuing popularity of the word 'multi-cultural' against these other words has, however, nothing to do with its exact meaning, and everything to do with the resonances of the word 'culture' and the positive connotations it evokes. If 'race' is now a suspect word, 'culture' by contrast is a vaunted, celebrated one, still strongly associated emotionally and nostalgically with a distinctive way of life which, despite all its deficiencies, speaks directly to an individual's sense of identity and belonging. And pre-cisely because individuals recognize in themselves the emotional charge which this sense of distinctiveness conveys, they are also prepared to recognize the significance and importance of the notion of culture in the lives of others. (This perception is what underlines the moral philosopher Charles Taylor's (1994) notion of the poli-tics of recognition in his writing on multiculturalism and identity.) What the word 'multicultural' does, then, which is different from the other terms mentioned is to create not just a sense of differ-ences but also to recognize those differences as springing from a universally shared attachment of importance to culture and to an implicit acknowledgement of the equality of all cultures – Harvey (1996: 70, 79) discusses this 'anodyne' aspect of the concept very incisively in relation to Europe. This last point, as we shall see, is taken up in animated political and philosophical debates, but for the moment I simply want to indicate this dimension of positive evaluation and implicit egalitarianism which multiculturalism hints at, since it is these aspects of the word which lead immediately to its adoption in educational circles.

If a nation is a multicultural society and a person's sense of self-worth is intimately and unavoidably bound up with their cultural identity, then the state, if it wants the nation to survive, can do one of two things. It can try to destroy the multicultural dimension of the society by rooting out all cultures other than a single one which will become dominant. At the extreme this leads to the kind of genocide with which tragically we became all too familiar in the twentieth century after the events of the Holocaust, the ethnic cleansing in the former Yugoslavia and the massacres in central Africa. (For a very good overview of genocide in this perspective, see Mann 1999.) This pursuit of a monocultural society can, however, take a more benign form through a policy of what is sometimes labelled 'coercive assimilation' by means of which, through employing the institutions of the state – schools, the legal system, qualifications for citizenship – other cultures are suppressed or persuaded to wither away and the dominant culture eventually becomes the only culture. In one way or another such a strategy has characterized the policies adopted by many apparently liberal democratic states through at least the first sixty years of the twentieth century, and this position, as Wieviorka (1998: 894–900) demonstrates – although it is not one which he shares – has a respectable pedigree associated with Republicanism on the French left.

The alternative to any attempt to create a monocultural society is to celebrate and encourage multiculturalism in the expectation that citizens who are proud of their culture and see that culture being endorsed by the state will be anxious to join in common citizenship with members of other cultural groups to protect the liberal tolerance which is so important for them. In such a perspective the enhancement of a sense of local belonging and an awareness of diversity paradoxically encourage a strong commitment to national goals and institutions. The term 'integration' is frequently used to distinguish this policy from one of assimilation, but it should be observed that there is still a confusion surrounding the two terms, with 'integration' occasionally employed to suggest assimilation (Grillo 1998: 177; and, for a German example, White 1997: 759) and 'assimilation' itself used to mean a benevolent incorporation of diversity within the unity of the nation.

One helpful way to understand the different thinking underlying these two strategies for dealing with the existence of several cultures within the nation, and one which has become a commonplace, is the analogy of the melting-pot to refer to the process of assimilation.[2] Originally coined by the Anglo-Jewish writer Israel Zangwill in his play of the same name, produced in New York in 1908, the term referred to the manner in which immigrants who came to the United States at the end of the nineteenth century were encouraged to think of themselves as Americans, gradually abandoning their cultures of origin until, as in the action of the melting-pot, they eventually became fully a part of the bright new alloy. Through a process of assimilation, then, facilitated by the state, all develop into Americans sharing a single common culture. Not only was this of course intended as description of what was occurring in the USA, it was also, in the light of social philosophy at the time, the desired outcome for which successive governments were trying to draw up a blueprint.

By contrast, when in the period from the late 1960s onwards social philosophy began to change and doubts were cast on not only the descriptive power of the analogy – clearly different cultural groups were not simply abandoning their original cultural characteristics – but also its desirability, the analogy which emerged to take account of the new circumstances was that of the salad-bowl. In the bowl different constituents retain their distinctive flavours and forms but the dish as a whole is recognizably *sui generis*, having its own distinctive character as a result of its unique blending. Culinary metaphors can, however, be taken too far, and there is a potentially disturbing dimension to the thought of social groups being tossed around like salad ingredients by governments simply concerned with flavours; nevertheless, this comparison of the melting-pot and the salad-bowl helps us both to imagine the difference between assimilation and integration and, by extending the analogy, to appreciate the positive advantages which contemporary governments hope to gain from celebrating rather than suppressing diversity.

This shift towards an endorsement of multiculturalism has not of course occurred uniformly throughout the world and, as we know, is still rejected by nations which feel that their fragile unity is threatened by demands for cultural equality from minority groups. With regard to the USA and Britain, however, we can see the shift as having taken place in the mid-1960s, albeit for different reasons in each case. In the USA it was a consequence of the civil rights movement and a perception of the strong and sincere emotions which underlay the black power campaigns that liberal Americans gradually understood the importance of allowing all American citizens the space and opportunity to build a foundation for their self-respect on the bedrock of their own cultural traditions. In Britain it was the novel experience of large numbers of immigrants from countries known as the 'New Commonwealth' who, while committed to the laws and norms of the society at large, saw no need to abandon their religious traditions or their cuisines or their languages, which led to a realization that assimilation was not the only means of incorporating immigrants into the society and that integration offered a more practical way forward, as well as a more liberal and ethically acceptable one. In both cases this led to a major change of orientation in educational thinking.

There was, however, a time lag of about a decade before this new realization was acted upon – although there was recognition of a need to render a positive account of other cultures and religious traditions, this recognition was not coupled with a perception that practical steps would have to be taken to pursue this policy and one could not simply depend on calls to the public at large to be more broad-minded in the hope that something would rub off. When at last this understanding did filter through, its first impact was in schools, where room was made on curricula to explore the origins of the diversity to be found in British and American society, and teachers were encouraged to see the presence of children from ethnic minorities in their classroom as both a challenge and a resource (Grillo 1998: 179). Not all these initiatives were a success, and there has been criticism of the tokenism (Brah 1996: 229) of many of these early attempts to introduce what became known as multicultural education, but the general thrust of the new policy, predicated as it was on a strong notion of social justice, went unchallenged: a multicultural curriculum simply reflected the new multicultural society of the second half of the twentieth century.

As these debates about the curriculum and education developed, however, the original, relatively innocuous, descriptive use of the adjective 'multicultural', and of 'multiculturalism' as the noun derived from it, gradually began to generate a different usage which

had political and philosophical dimensions and was far more controversial. The expansion of the term arose partly from the changing political climate in international politics in the late 1960s and
1970s and partly out of the debates surrounding minority rights and
the feminist movement. In Europe and the USA this was the period
of the so-called 'second' post-war wave of international migration,
giving rise to a new set of social and political issues requiring a
thorough review of government policies.[3] In other parts of the
world, among the most dramatic of the events of the period one can
recall the expulsion of Asians from East Africa and the exodus
from Vietnam of the boat people, as they became known, who were
largely members of the ethnic Chinese minority. Here in both cases
the dominant ethnic majority was seeking to expel or discriminate
against an ethnic trading minority which had been established in
the country for generations. The effect of these actions was twofold.
First, it led to a reopening of the debate in the international arena
about the rights of ethnic minorities and the position of their
culture within the country in which they had been settled for generations, with ominous echoes of similar debates about the Jews in
Germany. Second, as these expelled minorities came to settle as
refugees and immigrants in Britain, the USA, Australia, Hong
Kong and Malaysia, the practical problems of accommodating them
brought home to the host-country governments and the relief agen-
cies the immediate need to understand ways of life, patterns of
kinship and family organization, and moral values – in short, cultures – which were very different and could not simply be absorbed
and transformed to fit into existing institutions. This frequently
gave rise, for example, to anxious debates about whether it was
better to house the new immigrants together in specific locations in
the country where they would be able to call on each other for
support, with the risk that that might lead to the ghettoization of
the community, isolating them from mainstream society and risking
the spiral descent into poverty traps which had befallen other
minorities; or whether the strategy should be to split up the
refugees so that they would be quickly absorbed and assimilated,
but with the risk of possible psychological trauma as a consequence
of the isolation from their community. Such debates then quickly
led to more general discussions in the society at large about the
degree to which the state should protect or actively support cultural
difference and not just, as it were, celebrate that difference by
simply tinkering with the school curriculum.

The issue of the rights of ethnic minorities, which were initially regarded – at least after civil rights legislation had been passed in the USA – as again essentially a problem of countries of the South where democratic principles were unstable if not non-existent, was also taken up with a vengeance in the countries of the North. In the USA, for example, it was clear that not only was the black population the object of discrimination but so too were the native Americans and the Spanish-speaking minorities. In Australia the plight of the aboriginal people which had always been a relatively under-discussed topic became a heated issue. In Britain the demands of those advocating independence or separate status for Wales and Scotland, previously confined to an eccentric fringe, now merited serious consideration. The question of separate political status was an even more significant issue in Canada, where separatists in Francophone Quebec were making a temperate and well-reasoned case for independence predicated on a separate cultural identity of which the use of the French language was the most visible component. In fact the positions adopted in these debates in Canada have led to some of the clearest and most lucid statements surrounding the politico-philosophical dimensions of multiculturalism so far (see Taylor 1994; Kymlicka 1995; and, for an interesting discussion of their views, Lamey 1999).

In the broadening of the concept of multiculturalism to encompass the rights of minorities, the feminist movement has frequently provided a model for the resolution of apparent injustice. However, one should note that, both in terms of conceptualizing the issues and in setting the agenda for what needs to be done, there has been a constant movement to and fro of ideas between feminists and minority rights activists and that parallels between them are no coincidence. An example of borrowing by the feminists is the idea of double consciousness taken from the black writer W. E. B. Du Bois (1868–1963), who used it to describe the way in which blacks in the USA had two perceptions of themselves – one which derived from their own community and its traditions, and the other from how they perceived the majority white population to regard them. As a consequence of this double consciousness, their lives were lived as a negotiation between those two perceptions, sometimes responding to the white gaze by acting in a way corresponding to its expectations, sometimes only seeming to, while at the same time guarding a sense of self-respect. Women, some feminists argued, responded in the same way to the male gaze and to a male-dominated culture.

Given the parallels in the way in which women and Asian and Afro-Caribbean ethnic minorities are configured by white male attitudes, it is not surprising that in radical debates in the 1970s and 1980s women and ethnic minorities would see themselves as being in very similar if not identical positions and that consequently they should employ each other's vocabulary with reference to equality of opportunity, affirmative action, proportionate representation and educational disadvantage. As a consequence, since what was at stake for ethnic minorities was a demand that the state recognize and support the value which they themselves placed on their cultures, the term 'multiculturalism', in the context of such debates, took on very sharply defined political connotations. Additionally, in the same way as feminism provoked a backlash, so too has multiculturalism. Both now find themselves on the same side in the debates over political correctness and its limits. To discuss these polemics here, however, would be to jump ahead of ourselves, and we need first to pause to examine in more detail how precisely the discussion on multiculturalism has become sharpened in the last two decades to reach its present position. Rather than deal with this abstractly, it is useful to take examples from the experience of several countries; at the same time as illustrating the different political, social and economic contexts in which multiculturalism becomes a matter of contention, this review will serve to demonstrate how globally widespread the issues are.

Let us begin with Japan, a country usually regarded as culturally uniform and ethnically homogenous. Most Japanese, it seems, while recognizing regional differences in Japanese culture – between, say, Osaka and Tokyo – would probably deny that there were disadvantaged ethnic minorities in the country, not through any misplaced defence of their country but simply through ignorance. The plight of ethnic minorities rarely surfaces in public debates. Yet it is undoubtedly the case that ethnic discrimination exists. It affects the Korean-Japanese in several ways in both public and private domains, determining for example their career prospects, their friendships from an early age, and consequently issues such as marriage partners and family life (Hicks 1997). Another minority group in Japan is the *Burakumin*, whose origins derive from occupational specializations established far back in Japanese history but who are still marked out in Japanese society as an inferior-status group. Not immediately physically or linguistically distinguishable from the majority population, their areas of residence are confined to specific quarters of a town or city, and when, as is the custom in Japanese society, enquiries are undertaken of an individual's family background in matters relating to marriage or employment, once *Burakumin* origins become known this leads to social exclusion (Wagatsuma 1968). These problems of minority rights had until the twentieth century been largely ignored in Japan, but for some time now there have been vigorous campaigns to bring the matter to public attention. At the moment, however, there seems to be a lull in the campaigning, partly as a consequence of the marked improvements in the conditions faced by Burakumin in the past three decades, and partly because of uncertainty about whether the government should adopt further methods to eradicate discrimination altogether or simply hope that things will continue to improve without further intervention (Neary 1997).

In China, where there exists a fierce pride in the traditions of the dominant Han ethnic group, there is an ironic twist to the debates on multiculturalism and the rights of ethnic minorities. Historically, as the Chinese empire expanded, various measures were taken to incorporate ethnic groups and their territories into the Chinese nation, sometimes, for example, by introducing the Chinese script where no written script or only a rudimentary one existed before – this, for example, was the case in Vietnam which China colonized for almost all of the first millennium AD. In other cases the Chinese pushed both script and language (Fitzgerald 1972). In all cases they tried to establish imperial bureaucratic institutions, and Han Chinese culture was seen as the model to which minorities should aspire (Hook 1991). Centuries of Han invasion and the ideology of Han cultural superiority and the myth of ethnic homogeneity – largely fashioned, it would appear, in the twentieth century by Sun Yatsen (Gladney 1999: 56) – have had the consequence that throughout China in the twentieth century, as modernization has occurred, ethnic minorities have, whenever possible, tried to pass themselves off as Han, in this way making a claim to superior status. Recently, however, there has been an unexpected reversal of this trend of Hanification (Gladney 1997). The Chinese government, apparently responding to criticisms that it has not allocated sufficient resources to developing the standards of living and the opportunities for ethnic minorities, has established a policy of economic support and special privileges for those claiming ethnic minority status, with funds being channelled to those groups. As a consequence, those who had formerly claimed to be Han or in some way assimilated into Han culture are now reidentifying themselves as a cultural minority with their own linguistic and historical traditions (Gladney 1991: 317).

One sees the operation of a similar principle in India where, however, the situation is complicated by the issue of caste or *jati*, often seen as a marker of Hindu identity. Ever since independence the Indian government, in line with the advocacy of Gandhi, has tried to act positively to promote the welfare of the untouchable population, some of them tribal non-Hindu ethnic groups, often referred to as scheduled castes and scheduled tribes and now by what is becoming their own preferred term, *Dalit* (Gandhi referred to them as the Harijan, children of God). Among them, too, there has been the same move to emulate those of a higher status while at the same time maintaining caste or tribal identities (Sinha 1967: 103). The Indian government, in trying to extend opportunities to these groups, in addition to granting certain economic privileges, now sets aside places in higher education for them. However, this policy has created a backlash from the middle-class castes who protest vociferously against what they regard as unfair discrimination against them, since their sons and daughters are now unable to win university places. In some cases it seems also to have led some groups to redefine themselves so that the government recognizes them as falling into the category of scheduled tribes.[4]

This phenomenon of redefinition or reassertion of a specific cultural identity in order to become eligible for new economic privileges is not confined to Asia. In Australia, for example, there has been vigorous contestation since the mid-1990s in relation to land claims made by aboriginal communities on the basis of cultural rights which have only recently become recognized as the basis of claims (see Kane 1997). In Canada a native American group recently successfully claimed a traditional right to whale-fishing and were thus exempted from the ban on whaling, even though their claim was denied by environmental groups who argued that whale-fishing had never been an element in the cultural tradition of these native Americans.

In many South American countries there are now strong movements of indigenous peoples who are engaged in creating an ethnic identity for themselves through a process which has been termed 'ethnogenesis' (Hill 1996), and in some countries they are able to mobilize themselves very effectively to win substantial concessions

from governments and make realistic demands for national autonomy within the state. A lot of the impetus for this new assertive-
ness derives from a strong historical consciousness of the process
of colonization to which they have been subject, a consciousness
which was further stimulated by the symbolic significance attached
to the 500th anniversary of Columbus's voyage of discovery. In this
context Whitten (1996) describes the impact of the *levantamiento
indígena* (indigenous uprising) movement in Ecuador both on
the consciousness of the indigenous populations themselves and
on the white population reacting to their demands. One of the
points which emerges from this discussion of the South American
examples is the way in which these local movements, thanks to
globalization and the dissemination of communications technology,
are not only able to link up with other groups within the country
itself but are also active participants in the world-wide campaigns
of indigenous peoples and have in common a specific vocabulary of
human rights which they employ in the framing of their demands.
This gives them a significant international credibility and at the
same time ensures a sympathetic response from human rights
activists throughout the world.

In addition to these questions of special privilege and legal rights
of indigenous minorities, however, another set of deep-rooted and
widely ranging arguments has emerged in countries such as the
USA, Britain and France, extending the debates about multiculturalism in a different direction. Although, as we shall see, there
are immediate political and social dimensions to these debates, it is
important to recognize them as deriving from a philosophical discourse concerning the foundations and principles of a European
democratic tradition. Prompted by the observation that there now
reside in the North large immigrant populations who derive their
religions and moral creeds from sources other than Christianity and
the ideas of the Enlightenment, the starting point of the debate is
a disagreement about the degree to which Western liberal ideas
should form the common core of values to which all citizens must
subscribe and should be the final arbiter in disputes about the distribution of justice.

Liberalism is a priori a creed of tolerance and intrinsically identified with certain freedoms – free speech, worship, equality before
the law – and is apparently neutral in its evaluation of other beliefs,
at least in so far as they do not threaten liberalism itself. This stance
of neutrality, in relation to non-Western cultures in particular,

appears to reach its culmination in the principle of cultural relativism, a belief that no single culture is better than any other and
that there are no transcendent criteria to which one can appeal for
justifying the imposition of one culture's norms on another. This
principle, however, gives rise to the quintessential liberal paradox,
as Ernest Gellner (1995) was never tired of pointing out with great
glee to all and sundry, including the great champion of liberalism,
Isaiah Berlin: if there are no transcendent values then liberal values
are themselves not transcendent, and if they are not transcendent
then there is no reason why we should accept the primacy of the
tolerance of relativism as a good in itself, and if that is the case then
we can reject tolerance; but liberalism insists that we accept tolerance, therefore liberalism is transgressing its own fundamental
principles. To argue in this black and white reductionist fashion is,
however, to fail to do justice to the complexity of arguments on the
ground for what seems to be a victory for rhetoric rather than substance – alas, a tendency to which Gellner was all too prone – and
volumes have been written to show that there is considerably more
to the liberal tradition than this argument would concede.

Nevertheless, even among strong advocates of liberalism there
are disagreements about the limits of tolerance, and these are
nowhere more evident than in the discussions on multiculturalism
which have emerged in the last two decades. At the nub of this
debate is a point made very forcefully by Bhikhu Parekh (1994), a
champion of liberalism in its universal form, that the liberalism so
frequently enunciated in the tradition stretching from Mill to Rawls
is a liberalism which fails to understand how deeply it is influenced
by Western values deriving in effect from an intolerance of non-
Western cultures. This is to over-simplify Parekh's point and we
shall consider it at more length later, but we can perhaps understand something of his position if we look briefly at some of the
more contentious public issues which have in recent times caught
the public eye in relation to multiculturalism and are the background against which he is writing.

When in 1987 the faculty board of Stanford University made a
decision that a core course in the undergraduate programme on
great books should be changed to reflect the range of world culture
and no longer be confined to Western classics (Gutmann 1994:
13–15), there was an immediate outcry. Two closely related objections were raised: first, whether there were any other cultural traditions which were as rich and sophisticated and therefore as worth

studying as the Western one; and second, whether, even if there were, it was not incumbent on those studying and residing in the USA to familiarize themselves with the Western tradition to the exclusion of others, since it was that tradition which was the foundation of the cultural, social, political and economic organization of the nation of which they had chosen to become citizens. The first objection was most succinctly expressed in a remark attributed to Saul Bellow to the effect that when it could be shown that the Zulus had produced works comparable to the writings of Tolstoy then he would read them. To those familiar with the history of British rule in India, the arrogance of the remark recalled Macaulay's Minute on Education of 1835 in which, in the context of discussing the appropriate educational policy to adopt towards India, Macaulay said that 'a single shelf of a good European library was worth the whole native literature of India and Arabia' (Brown 1985: 75).

The second objection spoke to more atavistic fears among some of the population that the dispute over the curriculum at Stanford was merely a further illustration of the way in which American values were being eroded by immigrant populations who, unlike their historical predecessors, wished to undermine the fundamental principles of American democracy. The government, they claimed, by making concessions to these new immigrants, according them special privileges such as affirmative action, quota places, and enacting policies allowing minority languages to be media of instruction in schools, had gone too far. Although in the interests of justice politically justifiable action had quite properly been taken on behalf of subordinate minorities – women, homosexuals, blacks, members of disadvantaged ethnic groups – this action had now been taken to extremes and 'political correctness' had gone too far. To their opponents this attack on political correctness and – with respect to ethnic minorities – the de facto attack on the integrity and value of non-Western cultural traditions simply illustrated the illiberalism of Western liberalism. In the ensuing polemics it was matters of public policy which most exercised those who became engaged in the popular debates of the time (which still continue unabated), but underlying public policy decisions there were larger philosophical principles in relation to theories of distributive justice and the rights of minorities, well summarized in Kymlicka (1995), which now took on a new urgency.

In France, even though as late as 1968 social scientists could say that the issues were not so grave as in other parts of the world

(Raveau 1968: 269), similar debates are now being conducted (Wenden 1991; Grillo 1998: 181–7; see also the useful summary in Ferenczi 1995), although they have been occasioned by different circumstances. Observing the settlement of Muslim immigrants in France from former French colonies in Africa over the past two decades the extreme right, led by Jean-Marie Le Pen, accepts the argument that coercive assimilation, the preferred policy of successive French governments, is unjust. People should not be forced to abandon their cultural traditions and their religious duties. Thus far the right shares common cause with liberal opponents of the government on the left. But then they part company. If, says Le Pen, the new immigrants wish to remain separate and to maintain an identity distinct from the majority population, they should be allowed to do so. By the same token, however, if the majority population, too, wishes to have nothing to do with the new immigrant traditions with which it has nothing in common, then for its part it too should not be coerced into mixing with or accommodating to these other cultures. In other words, what Le Pen is proposing here is a form of cultural apartheid which would also take the physical form of residential ghettos. Such an arrangement, according to Le Pen, would reflect the mutual contempt which each has for the other's culture. This is the politics of recognition with a vengeance. It is not of course a politics of respect, however, and this Gordian solution to the problems of defining an acceptable and equitable set of practices and principles reflects a worrying intolerance which has unfortunately managed to win the support of Islamophobe French intellectuals.

In Britain, too, it is the unaccustomed presence of large Muslim immigrant populations from South Asia in cities in the North of England and in the Midlands that has sharpened the debates about multiculturalism. The Rushdie affair, as it has come to be known, is perhaps the best-documented example of several public confrontations in large part orchestrated by the media. The Iranian fatwa calling for the death of Salman Rushdie for having insulted Islam in his novel *The Satanic Verses* understandably evoked storms of protest from liberal opinion, but in the ensuing and developing arguments the target of British liberal critical opinion became less the fatwa than Islam itself, and very rapidly – through a process of what Gregory Bateson (1972) has described, with great pertinence to issues such as these, as 'schismogenesis', where two sides, in their opposition to each other, through their confrontation accentuate the elements of their position which the other objects to – Muslims of even liberal sentiments found themselves vilified by the liberal press at its most bellicose. Since the high water mark of that period in 1991 tempers have cooled, but the liberal press, ever vigilant, has always kept a watchful eye on cultural practices which appear to transgress what it regards as British cultural norms – for example, the ritual slaughter of animals, the patriarchal power exercised by Asian men and the practice of taking children out of schools so that they can make visits to the family on the Indian sub-continent.

The controversies which have ephemerally flared over these media-reported issues have not yet had the same impact on academic debates as issues involving minority rights in the USA and Canada. In Britain the principal concerns taken up for debate by liberals and radicals alike have been questions of representation and freedom of speech rather than cultural lifestyles. The reason for this difference between the USA and Britain, or even between Britain and France, seems to derive from the relative ignorance of British intellectuals concerning non-Western cultures compared to their counterparts elsewhere. Thus, although liberals familiar with a discourse of class, gender and racial discrimination are only too happy to weigh into public debate with respect to equity and equality, they are much less sure of their ground on the issue of cultures: despite their claims, none of their best friends are Muslims. Cultural relativism as a critical standpoint consequently does not have the same purchase in Britain as elsewhere.

We shall be looking again in the chapters which follow at the British examples mentioned above as well as at the experiences drawn from outside Britain. The intention of this brief selective review was simply to demonstrate both the developing currency of the word 'multiculturalism' and how, in addition to its continuing usage as a descriptive term – 'Britain is now a multicultural society' – it is now used as frequently by champions and opponents to designate a philosophical and political position in relation to the future of global society. To opponents of multiculturalism, its advocates, influenced by extreme forms of cultural relativism and postmodernist denials of absolute positions, seem prepared to contemplate a future of anarchic chaos and intellectual paralysis, having abandoned the intellectual weapons of reason which once they might have deployed against the practices of the barbarians at the gate. As for the champions of multiculturalism, they are split between two camps – those who argue for an openness to other traditions and deny that this effectively means a surrender to relativism; and those who push for a more aggressive multiculturalism, seen as an incisive analytical tool through which to explore the asymmetries of power within nations.

As we have seen, the particular issues which give rise to the debates differ across national boundaries, as one would expect given the very different demographic and historical circumstances which have contributed to the distinctive character of each nation. Political, economic, cultural and religious matters differ in the salience of their hold on popular consciousness from one country to another. Nevertheless, there are clusters of issues which are common to the experience of more than one country, and the organization of the chapters which follow reflects this.

Chapter 1 takes the question of twentieth-century nationalisms and explores the degree to which multiculturalism has been perceived as a threat or an asset to nation formation and the creation of a national community.

Chapter 2 discusses the representation of other cultures for popular consumption through a nation's media and the way in which the state tries to impose its own account of how other cultures should be portrayed through direct intervention in the field of education. Central to this chapter is a general criticism (of the kind only to be expected of an anthropologist) that, from whatever country we take our examples, in the way other cultures are represented there is a tendency to reify and essentialize them, unfailingly portraying them as static and unchanging and as having a uniform effect on all those who are perceived to belong to these cultures. In no area is this more obviously the case than in relation to representations of religion which to be properly understood should always, like any other social phenomenon, be placed within an appropriate interpretative context.

Chapter 3 takes up the apparent paradox that at a time when the world appears to be shrinking and we are informed – admittedly by those who later seem to recant – that the end of history is fast approaching, distinctive cultural traditions appear none the less to be growing in strength, increasingly powerful and able to exert a leverage on the political processes.

Chapter 4, after preliminary remarks on the nature of the spread of cultural influence, retraces the history of responses to the settlement of immigrant populations in Britain and the USA in recent times and shows how attempts have been made to resolve this paradox of diversity in a time of apparent convergence.

Finally, a brief conclusion returns to the question of terminology and reviews the differential weight attached to the concept of 'multiculturalism' in its application to individuals and their life-styles on the one hand, and to nations and governments on the other, and ends with a cautionary note on the slipperiness of the word 'culture' when it is taken to mean a bounded set of definitive characteristics which are alleged to be the locus of a national identity. It also makes some suggestions about how we should understand the nature of cultural change and the implications of that understanding for the concept of 'multiculturalism'.

Notes

1 The word 'cosmopolitanism' has in fact very recently taken on a new lease of conceptual life with pretensions to extending the debate on multiculturalism, but in a manner which seems to me akin to 'soft' versions of the latter – see Vertovec (in press).
2 The French also have the same term, *le creuset français*, for their very similar view of the assimilation of immigrants into the nation (Ferenczi 1995).
3 Joppke (1996) offers an instructive comparison of attitudes in the USA, Germany and Britain in this period.
4 See Parkin (2000: 54–7) for a good summary of accounts of the shifting strategies in this respect of the Santal, a large tribal group in eastern India.

Nationalism and Multiculturalism

Multiculturalism and nationalism may not be intrinsically related, but it is certainly the case that in the twentieth century at least they have been awkwardly and dangerously entangled. An emphasis on the one has often meant a reduction in the importance attached to the other. In broad terms and allowing for exceptions, nationalism in most regions of the world was clearly more significant in the first half of the century: it was instrumental in persuading populations within the boundaries of one nation to mobilize against those of another, or, in colonial circumstances, to expel from within the nation dominant groups who owed their presence to military conquest in the recent past. It was only after the Second World War and decolonization in the 1950s that multiculturalism began to make its impact felt in Asia, Europe and America: national boundaries – with some critical exceptions – appeared to have become more or less fixed, and in the absence of political or economic threats states turned their attention to the maintenance of political stability and the encouragement of economic development. One way of generalizing from this global experience may be to say that an appeal to nationalism seems only capable of being a temporary expedient employed by political groups – governments, parties, movements – to create a sentiment of national unity, and that once the nation has been formed, the war won and the foreign rulers expelled, then within the nation, peoples – communities, classes, religious and ethnic associations – will begin to discover new foci as the source of their identity and self-respect.

However, although we can propose such an argument about the oscillations between nationalism and multiculturalism as a description of a common political phenomenon, we need to avoid the easy conclusion that the rhythms of these oscillations are everywhere the same. In fact the contrary is the case. Despite the twentieth-century global diffusion of concepts such as nationalism and their widespread uptake by diverse political factions, it is the very specific historical antecedents pertaining to individual countries which always determine not only the shape and form of subsequent sociopolitical developments – the character of the polity, for example – but also their direction and force – the contested objectives of the nation.

In what follows, this entanglement of nationalism and multiculturalism is examined in the recent experience of three continents, Asia, Europe and America, using the examples of Malaysia, Germany and the USA. In each country, as we shall see, it is the presence of recent immigrant populations – combined in the example of the USA with the growing self-awareness of internally colonized peoples – making legitimate claims for recognition which propel a debate on multiculturalism into the public arena. In each case, however, the particular socio-economic circumstances of the countries lead to distinctive policies devised to reconcile the apparently competing demands of national unity and multicultural diversity.

During the colonial period, roughly 1874–1957, Malaya was the classical example of what came to be known after Furnivall (1948) as a plural society, that is, a society which is a

> medley of peoples ... for they mix but do not combine. Each group holds by its own religion, its own culture and language, its own ideas and ways. As individuals they meet, but only in the market-place, in buying and selling. There is a plural society, with different sections of the community living side by side, but separately, within the same political unit.
>
> (Furnivall 1948: 304)

When the British first established a significant presence on the Malay peninsula what they found was not a nation but a number of independent Malay states each headed by a Muslim ruler. The population of these states consisted of aboriginal people still pursuing a hunter-gatherer lifestyle in the jungles, and indigenous Malays whose numbers were being constantly augmented by an immigrant population from Java and Sumatra which had no difficulty in integrating with the local populations. In addition, especially on the west coast in what were known as the Straits Settlements

– Penang, Malacca, Singapore – there were substantial trading communities of Arabs, Indians and Chinese, each of which, despite occasional intermarriage with the indigenous Malay population and the adoption of some of their dress and cuisine, maintained a distinctive cultural presence centred upon language, religious practices and kinship arrangements.

In order to take full advantage of the favourable international climate of opportunity which Malaya with its natural resources – rubber (successfully introduced from Brazil via Kew Gardens) and tin in particular – was well designed to exploit, the British from the early years of the twentieth century tried, with varying degrees of success, to streamline the political administration of the region by bringing the separate arrangements made with the different states under one rubric, and thus began embryonically to create the nation. At the same time they instituted a complementary division of labour among the different ethnic groups now to be found there. The Malays were to be the backbone of agricultural development, managing rice production and engaging in the production of small-holding rubber. The large rubber estates, owned and managed by expatriate companies, were to be worked by Indian labour recruited from south India. The Chinese, who had been encouraged to come to the peninsula in relatively large numbers and were now well established, could be happily left to develop the urban areas and commercial centres through providing retail and catering services and some skilled labour. The business of government and administration was to be conducted by British colonial officials aided by those members of the Malay aristocracy who had been co-opted into government and given a privileged education. As a consequence of this system of functional complementarity, each group remained physically and socially separate, in different residential areas, in different professions and following different systems of schooling. They were also prevented from any but superficial communication with each other by profound language differences. The only arena where they came together, as Furnivall notably remarked, was the market-place where they exchanged products but remained apart.

This type of colonial segregation was a relatively common phenomenon within the colonies of the time. One has only to think of East Africa, where the South Asians took on the role performed by the Chinese in Malaya, or the establishment of immigrant populations in some of the islands of the Pacific. What makes Malaya, such an exemplary case is the transparent and visible manner in which this pluralism was created and sustained until well after the colonial period. Given the way in which each community was encouraged to plough its own furrow, and in particular the fact that the majority Malay population was confined to rural areas where they remained largely in ignorance of the bigger picture developing in the country as a whole, let alone of developments in the international arena, it is hardly surprising that, *pace* occasional resentment expressed towards Arab and Chinese traders, nationalist sentiments were slow in developing. It was in fact only after the Second World War, when the British announced plans for decolonization in which they advocated equal rights for the indigenous Malays and for the immigrant communities, that an effective nationalism arose. It was at this point that the British-educated Malay aristocracy tapped into and fostered a sense of ethnic identity among the Malay peasantry. Ultimately, however, when independence did come in the late 1950s, the pluralist system established during the colonial period remained intact but with the addition of safeguards put in place to assure Malays of a privileged position within the state.

For a period of a little more than a decade, while the new nation established itself in the context of the political turmoil in the region – the cold war was at its height and being played out in Southeast Asia as fiercely as elsewhere in the world – political energies were channelled into ensuring the stability of the nation, now enlarged to include the former colonies of Sarawak and Sabah in Borneo (but having seen Singapore go its own way) and now renamed Malaysia. On 13 May 1969, however, coinciding with the end of Malaysia's confrontations with some of its neighbours and the setting up of the Association of South East Asian Nations (ASEAN), race riots broke out in Kuala Lumpur shortly after political elections, and it became clear that what had been regarded as an amicable arrangement among the different ethnic groups of the nation disguised deep-seated resentment. In the absence of external factors to which an appeal could be made to support the unity of the nation, measures had to be taken to recognize and deal with the potentially disruptive threats posed by multiculturalism, although this word itself was not used. How that issue was dealt with provides an instructive example of political engineering in a strong paternalist state.[1]

In effect the problem was dealt with in two stages, from 1969 to

1984 and from 1984 to the present, the division between the two stages being through no coincidence marked by the ascension to power of the present Prime Minister, Mahathirbin Mohamad. (For details of the policies adopted, see Lim 1985.) To begin with, the ruling coalition of parties which had been formed along ethnic divisions and was dominated by the large Malay party, UMNO, realized that it would have to do something to redress the economic disadvantages experienced by the Malay population. The situation as it existed was a curious reversal of that found in countries where it is ethnic minorities which labour under a disadvantage and where affirmative action has to be taken on their behalf, but it is common in precisely those ex-colonial countries described above where a pluralist system has been purposely constructed. It was perhaps fortunate for the Chinese in Malaysia – at least in comparison to their counterparts in countries such as Uganda, Burma and Vietnam, where trading minorities were expelled and their property expropriated – that their percentage size in the population, 35–40 per cent of 18 million, ensured that whatever special advantages were conferred on the Malays in terms of educational and economic privileges, their own position was politically relatively secure and the new economic policy which the government advocated, although not one with which they were completely happy, was one which they could live with. In addition, however, to simply making economic adjustments the government began to make strenuous efforts towards the creation of a distinctively Malaysian culture, something to which previously they had only given lip-service.

Two policies characterized this creation of a national cultural identity. On the negative side, cultural expressions of an identity which was non-Malaysian were frowned upon, making it difficult, for example, to obtain relevant permissions for theatrical performances, discouraging ties with China. On the positive side, the government invested in the promotion of Malay arts and crafts, encouraged the publication of literary magazines, set up competitions and literary awards and worked hard on museums and cultural exhibitions, and promoted a certain amount of royal pageantry – in brief, manufacturing a heritage industry well before a similar phenomenon became common in the North. Within a relatively short time there emerged a visible and colourful Malaysian culture, essentially Malay in origin, by which Malaysia could be identified. If all this might have seemed superficial window dressing to the ethnic Malays themselves, the government was prepared to act more tangibly to conciliate Malay opinion by, for example, constructing mosques and establishing a Malaysian national university which in its early years overwhelmingly recruited Malay students. The most significant step it took with respect to culture, however, which had nation-wide repercussions, was the enforcement of Malaysian (in effect the Malay language) as the national language, making it obligatory throughout the educational system and in government offices, replacing the ubiquitous English which had until then, despite Malaysian language campaigns, been the language of communication across ethnic boundaries.

This carrot and stick approach to getting across the idea of a common Malaysian culture had resonances with what was happening elsewhere in the region. It was exactly at that time that Lee Kuan Yew in Singapore was both trying to promote the notion of Singaporean identity and excoriating those who spoke of Singaporeans as Chinese. Both countries were attempting to establish a set of distinctive visible cultural markers by which citizens could identify themselves as specifically Malaysian or Singaporean. Whereas Singapore, however, was associating its national identity with an essentialized set of Asian or sometimes Confucian values, Malaysia emphasized the ethical dimension less and racial harmony more.

When Mahathir became Prime Minister in 1981 the danger of inter-ethnic violence had receded and, even though in the privacy of their homes people might still talk in a way which showed a certain contempt for the other, in public there was considerably more tolerance, and among students in particular there was a new healthy openness to each other's cultural lifestyles. Thus, though in private there might be little commensality among the different groups, in public gatherings, in office celebrations and even on the occasion of the major calendrical festivals – the end of Ramadan, Christmas, Chinese New Year – a tradition of inter-ethnic hospitality had developed. It appeared that once the significance of having a national public culture for the purposes of international advertisement had been universally acknowledged, then a certain degree of local ethnic display could be tolerated. Celebrations of religious ritual were especially innocuous, since there was little risk that festivities would develop into triumphal celebrations of communal identity of the kind previously witnessed in election victory marches in 1969.

After Mahathir's accession to power the imperative changed

from one of inward to outward focus. Now fully incorporated into networks of the new world economic order, and having to compete for the attention of global capitalism with its immediate neighbours among the tiger economies of the region, an even greater effort was required to convince all Malaysians that there was nothing to be gained by being parochial and everything to be played for in making a commitment to the modernization of Malaysia. To demonstrate this shift of direction, funds now went into national prestige projects – a national car (the Proton Saga), an inter-nationally acclaimed new bridge, new dam projects, and most recently a lavish new airport, with the promise of a new capital city and the most advanced information technology facilities in the region. Contemplating these developments, the ethnic Malays have sometimes felt that the hard-won gain of recognition of their special position within the polity has been sacrificed in this process: there has been a downsizing of the royalty, for example, and Mahathir has said that English may now be reintroduced as a medium of instruction in tertiary education. On balance, though, Mahathir has been able to command considerable support for what are regarded, despite the costs to the economy, as real Malaysian achievements, although some authoritative commentators are less positive about the response to Mahathir's initiatives than I am (Jomo 1989: 36–41).

With the nation united behind Mahathir's vision of the year 2020 when Malaysia will be one of the leading industrial nations of the world, what, then, are the consequences for multiculturalism? If, in the first place, we limit the term to its meaning of the coexistence of different ethnic groups each with its own cultural lifestyle, then Malaysia, at least as far as its major towns are concerned, has all the appearances of a thriving multicultural society. Indians, Chinese, Malays, Eurasians, Asian and white expatriates, men, women, children alike, each demonstrating their ethnicity or their preference for global styles in their choice of dress, move easily together around the inviting shopping malls of Kuala Lumpur, stopping to gaze at the same shopfronts and eating at the same pizza or fried chicken takeaway outlets. Outside in the streets the relationship between ethnicity and occupation makes economic divisions easier to perceive. Bookshops and clothes stores, although employing representatives of all groups, indicate by the prepon-derance of Indian staff in senior positions and the names of the shops themselves that they belong to Indian-Malaysians. Con-versely, by the same tokens many of the larger retail shops are clearly in Chinese-Malaysian hands. Restaurants each have their own ethnic clientele, with the exception that one will see in the Indian Muslim establishments some Malays. Cinemas show largely Western films, but in the video stores and music shops one will find a variety and choice reflecting each group's fondness for a musical style and a dramatic performance which go along with their mother tongue and its associated traditions. From time to time the loud-speakers from local mosques will broadcast the call for prayer and men dressed in sarongs and carrying prayer-mats walk slowly towards the mosque. They will stroll past small Indian stalls selling colourful garlands of aromatic flowers to be used for private worship at shrines in the home or in the temples. The familiar pictures and posters of Hindu gods and goddesses, found throughout the world wherever there are Hindu communities, can be seen for sale here too. The Chinese stores catering for the religious needs of the Chinese community sell candles and joss-sticks of all sizes as well as the accompanying paraphernalia, lucky rectangular red paper packets inscribed with Chinese ideograms and paper models so important for the mortuary rituals in Chinese custom. All these sights, smells and noises, very much taken for granted by Malaysians themselves as constituting their familiar everyday reality, strike the observer as abundant evidence of an easygoing multiculturalism within the context of a vibrant and successful modern economy which other countries can only aspire to.

The astute observer may well, however, pause to ask, as she asks about similar scenes in Singapore, whether appearance does not in this case mask the realities of an authoritarian state controlling very carefully the limits of both the expression of ethnic identity and the voicing of dissenting political opinions (for details of this control, see Seow 1994). To what extent, she may wonder, does multi-culturalism as a political project find support in the state's current political thinking? The responses one might make to this question are not straightforward and are difficult to insert into the frame of seemingly similar discussions elsewhere, which at first sight seem familiar but are in fact different. This caution itself, however, appears to be a slippery evasion, a prolegomenon to a defence of essentializing particularisms. One knows only too well that there are politicians who seek to deflect criticism away from dubious poli-cies by the specious claim that Asian values do not allow assess-ment and evaluation on the grid of so-called universal values. The difference in the argument here, however, depends on a perception not so much of cultural essentialism as of the dynamics of changing historical circumstances and the observation that the debates on multiculturalism are still too recent and too limited in their anthropological range to merit any confidence in the universal applicability of their propositions. At best, multiculturalism, when it is used as a term for identifying and analysing the characteristics of plural societies, is a heuristic concept to be tested against the reality of situations in different countries with an appropriate open-ness to the contrasting accounts of individuals and groups on what they seek from government and society. With this caveat in mind, then, let us return to the specific nature of multiculturalism in Malaysia.

The first point to deal with is the absence of any term for multi-culturalism, either in a form phonically adapted to the Malaysian language or in translation. This is not because it would be difficult to translate – the word *pancabudaya* might do the job well – nor because the intellectual and academic context in which to place the term does not exist. Comparable terms such as *pasca-penjajahan*, post-colonialism, are very much part of the repertoire of intellec-tuals in Malaysia, and the thinking of writers such as Edward Said and Samuel Huntingdon (1993) is familiar to scholars, politicians and journalists. The reason for the absence seems to lie more in the fact that the new coinage in English – designed as it has been to reflect the changed circumstances and perceptions of countries of the North coping with the expansion of new immigrant communi-ties and a corresponding expansion of the debate on rights – does not, despite appearances, address the issues which countries like Malaysia have been dealing with from a much earlier period. In other words, the problematic of pluralism, to revert to the older word, does not fully overlap with and is not superseded by multi-culturalism.

In Malaysia the debate is conducted, and has been for some time, in terms of a dichotomy between *bumiputera* (autochthon-ous, children of the earth) and non-bumiputera. As bumiputera, the aboriginal hunters and gatherers, the indigenous populations of East Malaysia and, above all, the Malays are accorded rights not granted to immigrant populations, and when the first phase of the affirmative action was undertaken in the period after 1969 this special privileging rankled with non-bumiputera groups, though open discussion of the issue was proscribed. In the second, post-Mahathir, stage, as the effects of affirmative action began to be felt and as the presence of a well-educated Malay middle class became fully entrenched in the political economy of the nation, the rhetoric of bumiputera/non-bumiputera, although not disappearing altogether, seemed to decline in significance. Partly, as we have seen, this occurred as a consequence of Mahathir himself emphasizing Malaysians over Malays, but very largely it was a product of the new economic circumstances of prosperity for all which led to a redefinition of goals and ambitions.[2] The symbols of Malay bumiputera identity simply ceased to carry the ideological weight which they had in the past. There are various reasons for this, too complex to develop here at length but including a new focus on Islamic ideals and a consequent abandoning of discussions of recent Malaysian history except among a small group of academics (Watson 1996a).

Parallel to this move away from bumiputera rhetoric has emerged a new orientation to a larger community beyond the nation, in the first place looking to the region and making common cause with the other nations of ASEAN, with whose citizens Malaysians are encouraged to share a common sense of purpose: there are ASEAN youth forums, cultural gatherings and sports events, for example. On another level there have also been attempts, since 1997, to introduce into Malaysia broader notions of civil society, *Masyarakat Madani* in Malaysian, launched significantly by the government rather than by independent intellectual discussion. Coinciding with the development of these new ideological strategies, and very clearly linked to them, however, the dramatically changing profile of the Malaysian work-force – now heavily dependent on migrant labour from Indonesia, the Philippines and Bangladesh – is creating other pockets of resentment within the country which are alarmingly reminiscent of the xenophobic sentiments expressed against migrant workers elsewhere in the globe. And whereas civil rights organizations elsewhere have at least been allowed the freedom to voice their disquiet about detention camps and forced expulsion, the debates in Malaysia have been muted. It is a sign of the backlash against the greater openness that seemed to be emerging that, at the time of writing, the former Deputy Prime Minister, Anwar Ibrahim, who was responsible for launching the idea of *Masyarakat Madani*, is now on trial on what many regard as trumped-up charges, and that concurrently in another court an activist belonging to a non-governmental organization is also on trial for slandering the government by describing alleged ill treatment and abuses in detention centres. As might have been anticipated, this backlash has occurred during a period of severe economic retrenchment which has once more turned the nation in on itself.

I have dwelt on the Malaysian example at some length because I wanted to encourage readers to think beyond those conceptual paradigms which have emerged from the very publicly aired debates which take the experience of the USA as their point of departure. Since the usual ways in which we think about multiculturalism have been largely shaped by our familiarity with the issues which have come to attention in the context of events in the USA and the countries of northern Europe, we need to be reminded that there are other perspectives on multiculturalism which we should bear in mind, otherwise we risk failing to distinguish between what is contingent and what is substantive in the nature of multicultural society. For example, one feature which emerges from the Malaysian case is the relative insignificance of the issue of history. The Malaysian government has, as we have seen, over the years created a Malaysian identity through *inter alia* stressing cultural heritage and historical tradition, and there can be no doubt that there is a popular version of that history with which most people in Malaysia are conversant. However, it impinges rarely on the active consciousness of individuals and in no way affects their perceptions of themselves or inspires their everyday actions. In this respect Malaysia is very different from its neighbour, Indonesia, where I would argue that history actively informs contemporary consciousness at a local and national level as a consequence both of a formal educational syllabus, which has always given a major place to civics and history, and the liveliness of an oral tradition.

This difference between Malaysia and Indonesia mirrors a similar contrast between British and American experience. A popular history of Britain – what Raphael Samuel (1994: 3–48) called 'unofficial knowledge' – is widespread though superficial, but rarely informs public attitudes and actions. A knowledge or at least a collective memory of the Second World War is a partial exception here. (As some German observers have argued, the war still seems to have a strong grip on the imagination of the British population and affects their perceptions of Germans.) Others – and I shall be developing one aspect of this argument later – might also want to make a case for the continuing influence of the images of empire on the way in which the public imagination both interprets the

contemporary realities of the developing world and colours under-
standings of ethnic minorities now well established in Britain
(Rushdie 1991: 87–101). Certainly there are strong grounds for
recognizing the importance of history in these instances, but these
exceptions aside, and *pace* the attempts of successive governments
since the early 1980s to change the situation through prescription of
the curriculum, a historically informed consciousness plays no direct
role in the everyday affairs of citizens. In the USA the situation is
otherwise. There, as in Indonesia, the whole public ethos is imbued
with a sense of history constructed out of well-honed chronological
landmarks and an accompanying set of cultural and ideological
milestones, reference to which evokes strong emotional resonance
for the population. The immediate effect on the consciousness of the
American citizenry is, as we know, a pride in the nation, sometimes
bordering on arrogance and leading to a supercilious posturing
towards other countries. At the same time, however, it should be
noted that the very self-righteousness of the account has provoked
reactions and is vigorously contested by minorities, native Americans and blacks in particular, who claim they are misrepresented or
ignored.

The Malaysian case, besides providing an illuminating example
of the complexities of one multicultural situation, has alerted us,
then, to the differential impact of a historical consciousness on the
construction of nationalist sentiment. It has also illustrated how colonial policy in the twentieth century, by determining the status and
economic positioning of immigrant populations, created a distinctive context for the subsequent debates about the cultural identity
of the nation. Germany, with very different historical antecedents,
offers a contrasting example of the negotiation between nationalism and multiculturalism. We might begin a comparison, however,
by observing some instructive similarities between Malaysia and
Germany. In the first place Germany, too, is a new nation, dating
from the unification, under Bismarck in the nineteenth century, of
several principalities. Here, too, although the machinery of unification was fuelled by military might and disciplined bureaucracy,
the ideological cement of the new national consciousness derived
from the philosophical anthropology of men such as Herder and the
brothers Grimm who had laid the foundations of a notion of the
German *Volk* with its own distinctive cultural traits, foremost
among which was the German language and its associated lore. This
stress on the language as a vehicle and symbol of German identity

became in fact so important a signifier for essential German qualities that one definition of German nationality was encoded in the
slogan *Ein Volk, soweit die Zunge reicht* – 'One people, as far as the
language reaches' (Puhle 1998: 259). Such an emphasis on lore and
language is exactly paralleled, as we have seen, in the development
of a Malaysian identity.

Both Malaysia and Germany also share common ground in
relation to the perennial problems faced by new nations with
respect to their constitutions and patterns of governance. In the first
place there is anxiety on the part of those in power about whether
the provisions for unification and unity will hang together and have
the desired permanence. This leads to a large measure of authoritarianism and an unwillingness to tolerate, certainly in the early
stages of modern state formation, any dissent or opposition. The
exigencies of government are declared to require a suspension of
the hallmarks and conventions of a liberal democracy allowable in
more established states. Second, the ideological rationale of the
state needs to be constantly shored up by significant reference to
culture, history and a sense of destiny in order, negatively, to suppress the creation of a space for airing alternative strategies for
development, such as religious solidarity, and, positively, to canal-
ize the newly released social political and economic energies as pro-
ductively and as synergetically as possible. In these respects we can
see an almost exact correspondence between the experiences of
Malaysia and Germany: the authoritarianism of the modern
German state matches the authoritarianism of the entrenched
coalition which rules Malaysia, and the references to a far-flung
German nationality and a German culture are uncanny echoes of a
distinctive Malay civilization in the diaspora which the Malaysian
government is currently at pains to advertise (Watson 1996b).

Having noted these similarities, then, we can now see the pecu-
liarities of the German situation in sharper comparative perspective. A useful start is to recall some familiar features of the German
discourse of nation, foremost of which is the distinction drawn
between German nationality and German citizenship. Partly as a
result of Herder's early formulations – or at least of the way in
which they were subsequently taken up – and partly as a result of
twentieth-century *realpolitik*, German nationality has always been
considered in the first place a matter of descent: Germanness is in
one's blood. In legal terms this is expressed as the application of the
ius sanguinis (right of blood), as opposed to the principle of *ius soli*

(right of territory), which confers a right of nationality through birth in a country, the principle followed by the USA, for example. Thus in this perspective, once a German, always – and wherever you may be – a German. This is as true of people of German descent in the USA and Australia as of those closer to home in Poland and Russia. This recognition of the principle of descent confers privileges on those outside the territorial boundaries of the state – for example, giving them the right of abode in Germany with accompanying rights of full citizenship. It also establishes a special interest on the part of German governments in Germans overseas. This has led to the observation that for Germans nationality is more important than citizenship (Puhle 1998: 265). (This explains, incidentally, why Hitler, even though not a German citizen, was none the less able to participate in German politics.) It also gives rise to some curious anomalies.

Migrants from Russia who settle in Germany but who speak a dialect of German unintelligible to Germans are considered nationals. Those from the former Democratic Republic (East Germany) are also of course fully German, the division between the two halves having never been recognized. However, second- and third-generation Turks resident in Germany and speaking fluent German are considered *Ausländer* (foreigners) (Horrocks and Kolinsky 1996: xv). In everyday life there arise common situations in which one fails to place an individual in an appropriate category because of difficulties with criteria (White 1997: 760–2). Language *per se*, as we have just seen, is insufficient, and since one does not demand to see a person's genealogical documents on first acquaintance one is thrown back on appearances. Thus the more Nordic one looks – blonde hair, blue eyes – the more one is assumed to be a German national, and conversely the darker one looks, the more one is taken for an outsider (Forsythe 1989: 144).

Even this category of *Ausländer* itself is curious. The term has two related meanings which are sometimes difficult to distinguish and which are indeed often deliberately confused. At one level, corresponding to the usage we have noted above, it simply refers to someone who is not German by nationality; on the other hand, it is also used in a more restrictive sense to mean something like 'not one of us'. In this meaning Germans see people from northern Europe as being one of them and therefore not *Ausländer*; whereas those from southern Europe, starting in Italy, are. These notions of who is a German and who is not operate on a sliding scale well summarized by Diana Forsythe (1989: 149) who describes how when, in conversation with Germans, she referred to herself as an *Ausländer* her interlocutors appeared to be irritated by her putting herself into what they regarded as an inappropriate category.

In short, then, we find notions of German identity formulated in the nineteenth century in the context of cultural Romanticism, and later amplified in darker periods of recent German history, still closely adhered to as a workable foundation on which to devise contemporary policies of citizenship and nationhood. As an aside here, we can note the striking similarity between German and Chinese views. The Chinese, too, have a strong commitment to *ius sanguinis*. Overseas Chinese, however long they have been settled elsewhere, still retain their Chineseness, though as in the German case there are problems with nomenclature. This is despite the Chinese government's reassurances to other countries that they urge those Chinese resident there to commit themselves fully to the countries in which they are resident. Moreover, as in the German case, overseas nationals subject to political persecution are encouraged to return to China, but once returned find themselves in an anomalous position. The East German problem, too, has its counterpart in the political status of Taiwan, which is not recognized as autonomous or independent by the People's Republic. The difference here, though, is that whereas East Germany was always economically far less developed than West Germany, the reverse is true of China and Taiwan.

Returning to the German experience, however, our interest lies not in pursuing the discourse of nation and race *per se* but in linking this to contemporary debates on multiculturalism, a word which, in contrast to Malaysia, has entered the political vocabulary and is currently the subject of much pointed discussion, with comparisons made with France and the USA (Milich and Peck 1998). One convenient point of entry into the new debates is the increasingly recognized absurdity of the often professed opinion that Germany is not a country of immigration – by which an implied contrast with the USA is intended – when set against the obvious fact of the immigration which has taken place since the early 1960s (Forsythe 1989: 153; Puhle 1998: 265). Not that there had not been immigration before then, but up to that point the numbers and the provenance of the immigrants – from central and southern Europe – could without too much difficulty be disguised.

The settlement of Turkish immigrants in relatively large numbers has exposed the pretence of ethnic homogeneity, and consequently there has arisen a need to deal conceptually with the issues in a way which will both win public support and conform to internationally endorsed liberal democratic principles (Joppke 1996). Hence the glance towards France and the USA, while retaining a sense of the special circumstances of Germany. A further factor to note here, however, is that the presence of Turks in Germany cannot be considered in isolation from the context of the global political economy which has given rise to that immigration and, most recently, made it highly problematic for some sections of the population. With the expansion of the German economy by leaps and bounds from the early 1960s came a demand for an industrial work-force which could provide the unskilled and semi-skilled labour which the Germans themselves disdained – shades of Malaysia inviting in Indonesians and Bangladeshis. Turkish immigration was encouraged, but the presence of *Gastarbeiter* (guest-workers), was initially perceived as a temporary measure to cope with a transient problem of labour shortage. Over time, however, the realization grew on the part of both the Turks themselves and the Germans that the Turkish presence had shifted to something permanent or semi-permanent. This appeared to be something which both parties were able to tolerate on the mutually acceptable understanding that for the most part Turks and Germans would remain culturally separate. There would no attempt of the kind that there was in France to encourage the immigrants to identify with the nation, that is, no coercive assimilation. Turks were of course encouraged to learn German and their children were obliged to attend German schools, but the thinking was that this learning of the language and increasing familiarity with the institutions of the state would only facilitate the contribution which the Turks could make to the efficient running of the economy. Turks were not encouraged to become citizens; on the contrary, they were tacitly persuaded to remain Turks. Dual citizenship was not permitted. Although this policy had the consequence of making the position of Turks vulnerable and uncertain – they could be deported at any time – on the whole they themselves, or at least the older generation, were satisfied with such an arrangement which allowed them to retain their Turkish identity while at the same time enjoying a reasonable economic standard of living.

In the course of the 1990s, however, the situation changed dramatically. As a result of the reordering of the capitalist economy two things have happened. First, the security of the labour force has disappeared. The new demands of the system mean that there are no jobs for life. The impact of this has been hardest on the middle classes for whom unemployment, so long banished from their imaginative horizons, has now reappeared. The spectre of unemployment in turn has led to a defensiveness and inward-looking orientation which has led to a search for scapegoats in the first instance among those who are not German: the causes of the present crisis, in other words, are attributed to the presence of *Ausländer*. This new set of labour arrangements, however, is in fact associated with another phenomenon which exacerbates the situation, the so-called 'Third-Worldization' of the First World (Ostendorf 1998: 55), in this case meaning the exporting of all unskilled and semi-skilled labour to the developing economies of the Third World with the consequence of creating unemployment in the First World. In the new scheme of things, then, the countries of the North tolerate higher and higher levels of unemployment – manageable through welfare payments – on the back of a high-skilled base of technologically sophisticated IT-led industries.[3] This new economic order, however, gives rise to unrest on the part of a German working class which finds itself unemployable. The Turkish work-force, as part of this semi-skilled class, is in the same position, and furthermore is not easily able to make the break-through to those white-collar jobs commensurate with the new level of educational attainment which they, as children or grandchildren of the original immigrants, may have achieved.

If the problem had remained at this level, containing the aspirations of Germans and Turks alike under the new economic dispensation, then it could perhaps have been resolved by the promise of relative economic security. This would have allowed the gradual accommodation of Turks and Germans to each other in the reworking of a notion of the national commitment and responsibility of the state to all its citizenry – this belatedly seems to be what the present government is attempting with its new legislation on citizenship, which accommodates many immigrant demands – but in fact the problem was compounded by German reunification and the economic costs which this entailed. There can be no doubt that after the initial euphoria of the destruction of the Berlin Wall a sober counting of the costs has led to an uneasy acceptance into the state of those former citizens of the Democratic Republic, who are now frequently referred to as the people of *Dunkeldeutschland* (dark

Germany). Furthermore, as might have been anticipated, with the reorganization of the eastern German economy and the elimination of its inefficiencies, major problems have surfaced as a consequence of unemployment among those who, even though they may not have had much in the past, did at least enjoy some job security. Their resentment at the failure of the new arrangements to live up to the promise which reunification in the abstract seemed to hold out to them has led to a backlash phrased once more in those terms of a German purity which are so shudderingly reminiscent of the Nazi past (White 1997: 762–4).

For their part the immigrants, still labelled as *Ausländer*, are no longer satisfied with the second-class status which that label implies and consequently require the state to redefine what constitutes the community of the nation. Thus multiculturalism in Germany now turns on the necessity of reformulating a notion of national identity which will both take account of the changing global circumstances in which national economies operate and at the same time recognize the contingency of earlier notions of German identity. The latter, despite the emotional appeals to a cultural essentialism, should be seen as the product of, at the most, a two-hundred-year phase of history determined by specific circumstances, in no way set in stone, and constantly open to redefinition in response to the demands of the present. The debates, however, have only recently taken on these new contours; and opinion still seems strongly divided in Germany itself and there is a long way to go before the government can be confident of having reached any democratic consensus.

What the German and Malaysian examples together demonstrate is that the struggle for the recognition of the status of a new nation requires the building up of a repertory of cultural characteristics – of which the most relevant are a language, a historical tradition and a set of tangible accomplishments, and of which the least well defined seem to be territorial boundaries – in which the people of the nation can take pride – since these characteristics come to constitute a large part of their personal identity, and which distinguish the new nation from others. In circumstances where the nation is vulnerable to external threats, or indeed labours under the domination of other nations – in a war or during colonial periods, for example – the appeal to a common purpose can serve to unite the nation. When, however, the threats are internal, as a consequence of economic decline or a sharp polarization of the economy, then popular sentiment looks quickly to the discrediting of minorities as an explanation of contemporary difficulties. And unless a government can build upon an existing multicultural tolerance within the society and move quickly to define common national goals and to root out this targeting of minorities – and in many cases governments do the opposite in the hope that by tacitly encouraging scapegoating they can displace criticism away from themselves – then cultural nationalism and xenophobia are likely to give rise to ugly incidents in which new immigrant groups become the victims of racist spleen.

A further point, not so far mentioned, which emerges from comparing Germany and Malaysia, concerns the apparent lack of commitment of the new immigrant groups to their own historical origins. Among the Turks in Germany it is the freedom to practise their religion which exercises them. With this freedom guaranteed, it is equality of economic opportunity which they look to next. In Malaysia, too, although ethnic minorities, the Chinese and Indians, conserve their own language traditions, they do not, on the whole, press hard for the state to recognize the status of their individual cultures through separatist legislation. Current institutional arrangements, as long as they safeguard economic opportunity and freedom of worship and provide scope for individual self-improvement, are deemed sufficient guarantees for the pursuit of the good life. In the USA, however, to which we now turn for our final example of the relationship between national and multicultural ideas, there exists a very different situation in relation to ethnic minority demands which are very different in quality, and quantity, and a consideration of the special circumstances which obtain there will help us to amplify our comparative perspective.

Among some American commentators, the manner and the extent to which minorities put their demands for special institutional consideration give cause for grave alarm, since they appear to be undermining fundamental principles of American national identity. For them affirmative action and political correctness have reached absurd proportions, to the point that they threaten the fabric of American society. Included in their condemnation is multiculturalism, which they also regard as emphasizing difference and separateness at the cost of national unity. The argument of perhaps the best-known spokesman on this side of the debate, the historian, Arthur Schlesinger, Jr (1998) runs like this. Until the 1960s, the notion that the USA was a country in which everyone shared a common belief in, and commitment to, American values, whatever their immigrant origins, was not seriously challenged. People came to the USA from very different parts of the world, bringing with them a variety of traditions and experiences, but once there they willingly embraced the American creed, a belief in the principles and philosophy of the Constitution, with its promise of opportunity for the individual. After two generations, with a knowledge of the language and an understanding of the history and traditions of the country, they became true Americans. The motto *e pluribus unum* ('from the many, one') was thus constantly being re-enacted. From at least the end of the nineteenth century, after the end of the Civil War, the sense of a distinctive American identity had been unshakeably established. Not that there were no dark spots in this triumphant progress of American ideals, as Schlesinger readily acknowledges. The treatment of black Americans, the terrible measures taken against American Indians and the restrictive legislation which discriminated against Asian immigrants are simply a few examples. Nevertheless, the principle of equality of opportunity had been laid down and it was simply a matter of time – till the 1960s, as far as black Americans were concerned – before its relevance to all Americans was understood and put into practice.

It is true, Schlesinger continues, that in the 1920s and 1930s there was some criticism, voiced by Horace Kallen – about whom see Grillo (1998: 190–4) and the illuminating chapter by Hornung (1998) – of the melting-pot ideal, to the effect that the moulding of everyone to the same Anglo-Protestant tradition was to be deplored and that more allowance should be made for diversity and difference, but this debate was largely academic and did not have much resonance among most Americans.[4] As for the Anglo-Protestant tradition, one has to accept that historically this tradition has lain at the core of American values and American society, and hence it is important to be aware of and study it. This does mean taking a canonical approach to American culture, but the substance of the canon is constantly changing and one should have no fears of ossification.

Now, however, according to Schlesinger, a change in orientation to the ideal of assimilation has taken place. The laudable campaigns for civil rights in the 1960s have led to an extremism which begins with a rejection of the American creed. Demands are now being made for a recognition of the separateness of ethnic identities.

Examples of this are separate language provision for Hispanic-Americans, the devising of new history curricula which highlight the accomplishments of individuals from ethnic minorities, and separate institutional arrangements for minorities in universities. The underlying rationale of all these demands is the need to take affirmative action to endorse the pride of ethnic minorities in their own history and traditions and thereby their self-confidence, so that they can compete equally with the majority in public domains. Although the desire to improve opportunities for those from ethnic minorities is commendable, this stress on difference is not the best way to do it, and in fact risks exacerbating the situation through divisiveness which creates inter-ethnic hostility and undermines the principles of equality which for so long have worked to make America the envy of the world in terms of multiethnic harmony.

Put this way and with liberal use of numerous examples of what appear to be absurd practices, the arguments of Schlesinger and those whose illustrative examples he relies on, people such as Dinesh D'Souza, give the appearance of eminent reasonableness. By showing the ridiculous measures introduced to satisfy the demands of advocates of multiculturalism they successfully, in their own eyes at least, drive another handful of nails into the coffin of political correctness. Or so it seems. The problem with arguments of this kind, however, so heavily dependent on letting extreme examples do the work of substantive debate, is that they fail to understand fully the issues at stake and mistake contingency for substance, a situation which becomes compounded when, on the other side, a defence of examples is mounted at the expense of clarifying the principles at stake and steering the discussion in the direction of issues of power and justice.

In fact there are several different issues among the many points which Schlesinger raises which, if they are to be properly reviewed, need to be treated separately. The first, and the one we are most interested in here, concerns the relationship between multiculturalism and nationalism, specifically in this case the question whether an American identity is compatible with the coexistence of different cultural traditions, each competing for equality of treatment within the nation, or whether a commitment to the nation, which immigrants make when they take on citizenship, requires the dissolution of differences into a homogenous unity. A second issue is how to redress the injustices to which blacks and native Americans as collectivities have historically been subject. A third is how to create, through a set of policies, equity and justice for those individuals who because of their membership of disadvantaged groups – not just ethnic minorities but the underclass of a society, women in certain circumstances, gay groups, the disabled and members of non-Christian religions – suffer discrimination and are consequently unable to share in opportunities for full enjoyment of the benefits of civil society: policies which, in other words, will deal with the problem of social exclusion. Another issue altogether is the critical evaluation of cultural traditions and the most appropriate forms which a syllabus of liberal education should take, both in schools and universities. Included here is the question whether a syllabus should be confined to a set of books and arguments which are identified with a single canonical tradition. Conflating these issues in the interests of brevity leads to confusion, and, rather than follow Schlesinger's example, I want to confine the discussion here to the first of the issues mentioned above, the compatibility of nationalism with multiculturalism or, as Schlesinger himself puts it, the *unum* with the *pluribus*.

It is significant that the challenge to what seems to have been for so long the taken-for-granted notion of American national identity comes at a time when that identity has already been securely in place for almost a century. In this respect we see at once a major difference from the situations in Malaysia and Germany where, as we have noted, the idea or image of the nation is still in the process of consolidation. In the latter cases we would hardly expect challenges from migrant communities to be phrased in terms of opposition to the cultural identity of the nation since the latter is still embryonic and – despite the claims of ideological myth-makers – mutable. Instead what we see is a demand that the state simply keeps abreast of the rapid global changes which are affecting the day-to-day lives of the citizenry and makes the necessary accommodations and adjustments in the legislative domain from time to time. The situation is very different in the USA where, as Schlesinger takes pride in noting, there has been until recently a general satisfaction with definitions and conceptions of what constitutes America.

It is, however, precisely this observation of a long-held general satisfaction, seen often as smugness and complacency, which gives rise to the scepticism of those who advocate a rethinking of Americanness: the failure of the nation to contemplate a change in its self-image, when all around is changing, smacks of hubris and dogma rather than of reliability and good sense. In order to unsettle that complacency, advocates of change point out how the present situation, unlike that of a hundred years ago, is no longer containable by appeals to the American creed: a notion of simple distributive justice requires us to remedy the deficiencies of the contemporary situation. It is justice which demands that the descendants of those black slaves and those native Americans who were the subject of so much violence by the state be given special consideration, not simply because they are descendants but because the consequences of that violence still affect individuals today in terms of preventing them from taking full possession of their lives within civil society. This is a proposition which Schlesinger seems to deny, arguing that the legal and constitutional principles are already there in place allowing all to share the American dream unburdened by who their ancestors were or how they suffered.

In the second place, the special needs of non-white Anglo-Protestant immigrants, especially those settled in the second half of the twentieth century, have to be addressed. Here the argument from justice is more difficult to sustain, and some political philosophers (for example, Kymlicka 1995) have drawn a distinction between those groups like the blacks and the native Americans who were the subject of state violence, and those immigrants who chose voluntarily to come to the USA and through that free act implicitly accepted both the obligations of being citizens and the philosophical creed and culture on which the state was based – in other words, the principle of *e pluribus unum*. Against this run counter-arguments which turn on precisely what it is that immigrants from persecution or poverty are acceding to. In this context one might point more generally to a new anthropologically sharpened awareness of the conditions required for the realization of human dignity, conditions which include the right to know and explore one's cultural heritage – as well as the right to reject it. Consequently, the requirement to forget the past and one's cultural origins, the very foundations on which one constructs a sense of self and identity, is repressive and unjust and an improper demand for a state to make.

I imagine that very few would deny the validity of the general argument phrased in this fashion, but the battles which rage over the issue of political correctness rarely begin from this premise but instead, as exemplified in the various polemics, focus on particular policies and actions which are regarded as ends in themselves. We shall discuss some of these issues as they relate to educational policies later, but for the rest of this chapter let us look at the idea that a concession to the demand that minority cultures be institutionally recognized will ultimately mean opening the door to division and cleavage – in effect, as Schlesinger puts it in the title of his book, 'the disuniting of America'.

The fear for the loss of a national culture – or national self-image, or national idiom, or national creed – springs from a strong conviction that one's own sense of self-respect, one's own set of moral values and political principles which one wants to pass on to future generations because these things are good in themselves, seem to be in jeopardy; the crisis of the nation is in this sense a personal crisis since one's own set of beliefs, and consequently one's self-esteem, are being implicitly denied – this, of course, is the argument of ethnic minorities in reverse. In fact the fear rests on a false premise of what a national culture is and how it affects individuals. Culture itself is a catch-all word, but let us not get entrammelled here in debates about its meaning and simply take it in this context to refer to a distinctive way of life which, when speaking of national cultures at least, is alleged to distinguish one nation from another. This is the sense in which it is popularly used when reference is made to British, French, American, Spanish, Samoan, Chinese, Indonesian cultures. And, if put to the test, people questioned on the substantive content of this culture can provide certain rough and ready definitional characteristics, though the set given in each case will differ according to who is being asked to define the culture or whether an individual is defining their own national characteristics or those of other nations. However, the point to note is that although these summations of national character may be widespread and in constant use, they are all spurious (cf. Parks 1999).

An easy way to test this is to ask oneself what are the common features, moral and political principles, cultural reference points, which one shares with all one's fellow countrymen. The more one thinks about it the more hard-pressed one is. Rather than a national heritage, it is socio-economic background, education, occupation and religion which have the stronger influence on behaviour and attitudes, and we can observe very easily how such influences frequently mean that, despite differences in language, we often have more in common with others across national boundaries than within them. If one nevertheless persists in a search for national characteristics which are distinct, one either ends with the banal and the trite – support of national sports teams, a sense of fair play, roast beef and Yorkshire pudding – or one makes reference to general democratic principles, the right to vote in elections, self-determination, equality of opportunity, all features which most peoples of the world would claim to be characteristic of their national cultures too in their ideal form.[5] Furthermore, any claim about the continuity of cultural forms would be found on close historical examination to be unsustainable, since in fact the symbols and forms of the culture have always been in a state of flux and have undergone substantial change over the centuries.

If, then, it is the case that national cultures and national traditions are, beyond a very superficial level, specious entities when compared to, say, national laws and national political institutions, where the term 'national' simply relates the issue of sovereignty, then how does this affect the debate on multiculturalism and nationalism? In the first place it should make us question the source of those strong emotions and attachments which, it was suggested above, we all to some degree feel in relation to the notion of our own native traditions. It may well be that what we are responding to is not at all a cultural tradition, let alone a national culture, but simply familiar institutions – what Durkheim called 'social facts', conventional ways of doing things with which we are so intimate that they are 'second nature' to us. Their very familiarity provides us with a psychological security, of the same kind as the use of our mother tongue, another 'social fact', and for that reason anything which is alleged to jeopardize their existence seems a threat to our own identity – or, to put it in terms of a well-known anthropological set of ideas, these alien elements appear to contaminate or pollute us (Forsythe 1989: 152). But this recourse to what we regard as familiar disguises the fact that we are constantly adjusting to changes in our social environment and learning to recognize new cues and how to act appropriately to them. Hence what we feel such a strong attachment to is not in fact a cluster of habits but the memory and evocation of that state of sureness and familiarity which we are persuaded by authoritative others – politicians, writers, media representatives, the personalities of popular culture – to refer to as a national culture – pegged to suitably powerful and resonant symbols such as the Union Flag, the white cliffs of Dover, state pageantry and heroic historical figures.

If we were more conscious of the way in which these appeals were being voiced we would be less likely to succumb to the seductive power of nationalist rhetoric and more inclined to interrogate the claims being made in the name of nationalism or national culture: beyond the appeal to the commonly shared polysemic symbols – which can mean different things to different people, while still carrying the same emotional weight for all – what are the values and the institutions which we are being asked to endorse, and are they in their present form as central to our identity as they appear to be for the advocates of a national tradition?

It may well be that when we have penetrated through the rhetoric of nationalism and tradition, there are values and perspectives and ways of doing things which we do share with advocates such as Schlesinger, but equally we may find ourselves coming to accept the styles of life and perspectives on the world which we have learnt through engagement with those whose origins and status in society are different from our own – and this would apply not simply to styles lived by members of ethnic groups other than our own but to those of a different class, occupational group or even gender. Rather than simply take for granted what we have passively received, we have to make values our own, and the way to do this is through discussion, openness and the exchange of ideas and the learning of new habits. And, of course, this is a two-way process: as those of us from the dominant majority learn from the minority communities around us through active engagement with their tradition through discussion and comparison, so too those of us within those communities learn to change in our way. The threat to the social fabric comes not from the challenge posed by seemingly alien traditions but from the refusal to engage in discussion, the unwillingness to contemplate change and the misperception of what culture is. That in fact this engagement is taking place and that, despite the attempt to preclude debate, there is argument and an exchange of opinions in the context of multicultural issues is a reflection of the health of an ongoing tradition, democratically open to change and transformation. It is not a cause for regret. As Hall and Lindholm (1999: 5) put it in their carefully argued response to the Jeremiahs prophesying the break-up of America: 'Negotiation, discussion, and argument are forms of conflict, but they are also signs of life'.

Although Malaysia, Germany and the USA differ so profoundly in their histories, and it is one of the principal contentions of this book that we should be wary of imposing criteria and judgements drawn from the experience of one country on to another – a tendency which we all too readily indulge as though there were some easy universal template which we could take from the experience with which we ourselves are most empirically familiar – nevertheless there are conclusions which we can draw from comparing the three countries.

In all three countries, as we have noted, multiculturalism is debated in the context of what is alleged to be a national culture which defines the specific character of the nation. The limits to which multiculturalism can be tolerated are perceived to lie at the boundaries of what constitutes the core of that national culture, the integrity of which has to be preserved if the nation is not to fall apart. However, we have seen that this notion of a national culture is predicated on a very dubious essentialism, a cluster of characteristics considered immutable to which ritual reference is made. This is to misconceive the nature of culture, which is constantly being remade and refashioned according to the exigencies of the moment. The nationalisms of all three countries have over the years emphasized very different features of traditions which comprise their collective experience. Malaysia in the 1950s and 1960s chose to stress the Malay monarchy as a quintessential feature of Malayness and therefore Malaysian identity, but now increasingly the monarchy is marginalized. Germany used to lay stress on a metaphysical concept of the spirit of its people (*Volksgeist*), and although, as we have seen, traces of an insistence on blood rights are still to be found, there is now a new emphasis on citizenry – even though the debate may be stuck half-way (Radtke, quoted in Ostendorf 1998: 53). In the USA, where the systematic effort to inculcate a set of cultural and historical reference points through the educational system has been so much stronger than elsewhere, the images of America have begun to change after the universal recognition of the sufferings of American blacks and native Americans. The former emphasis on the melting-pot now gives way to a notion of the salad-bowl.

Slow incremental modifications, as opposed to radical and rapid change, are not always obvious to those who live through them. There is no immediate sense that a transformation has occurred, and consequently there is a belief in something permanent and stable, and when this appears to be directly challenged – as in the case of the civil rights movement in the USA or feminism globally – there is initial dismay and resistance. When eventually proposals for changes are legitimized directly through legislation, gradually the justice of the earlier claims is recognized. In terms of national debates, what we are witnessing in the American case is a realization that although legislative measures and the constitutional rights of the individual are the necessary conditions to appease initial demands for equality, in the longer term a nation's view of itself must be broad enough to encompass different cultural experiences. Minorities must be allowed to contribute to that debate of what it is which constitutes the good life and how the state should assist its citizens to pursue that goal. In other words, the perception that multiculturalism and nationalism are doomed to be locked for ever in a battle for the soul of the nation's people dissolves once we understand that nationalism, being simply the political use to which a state puts a collection of ideas, is inherently a transient phenomenon with no substantial essence. The manner in which a mature sense of commitment to universally acceptable values grows is through exposure to other traditions beyond those with which one is familiar, since they constantly challenge us to review our concepts of what we should most value for ourselves and others.

Notes

1 I was at this point just about to write 'Asian democracy' instead of 'paternalist state' in order better to make a later contrast with Western democracy, but quickly decided against this since that would be falling prey to exactly that sort of essentializing of Asian and Western experience which I am usually at pains to reject. Malaysia differs from other Asian countries as much as one Western country differs from another.

2 Some writers (Lim 1985: 269; Nonini 1997: 207) have argued that though the notion of a Malaysian identity has strengthened, there is still considerable resentment on the part of the Chinese at being unable to promote their cultural heritage. I am less sure about this and feel that Mahathir's part-restoration of English as a medium of instruction in tertiary education has mollified some Chinese opinion while antagonizing some Malays.

3 See the remarks of Ferenczi (1995) on the relevance of this development to the French situation.

4 Another important voice of that time whom Schlesinger does not mention is Randolph Bourne (see Trommler 1998: 169, 181).

5 Where disagreement would arise is in the degree to which people find it acceptable for the state to dictate the limits of freedom of expression, some arguing strongly for minimal state interference and others arguing that such intervention is a necessary condition of freedom for all – in particular, for those who would otherwise suffer discrimination. See the remarks of the Malaysian Prime Minister, Mahathir (1996), in this respect.

Education, Religion and the Media

Schlesinger's attack on multiculturalism was largely prompted by and directed against changes which were taking place in the curricula of schools and universities in the USA as a consequence of lobbying from groups who felt that existing arrangements were weighted in terms of a model of the USA which was too Eurocentric. Indeed, it is this coupling of multiculturalism with a programme of educational reform which has more than anything else stirred passions in the American debates. The media appear to have been much more exercised by educational matters than, for example, by discussions of religious practice, which, as we shall see, are characteristic of debates in Britain and the rest of Europe.

Just why it should have been education which aroused such strong feeling in the USA can be readily comprehended once we recall that it is largely through formal education that Americans are socialized or inducted into a sense of what it means to be American. Precisely because of the diversity of the backgrounds of immigrants coming to settle in the USA, the family could not be relied on to be that repository of knowledge of American history and traditions considered an essential foundation on which to construct a pride in the nation and its achievements and a commitment to its goals. Individual families could be left to instil a moral sense in their children but they could not, unlike their counterparts in European nations, be expected to inculcate a reverence for those cultural and historical touchstones at the mention of which the pulses of all citizens should immediately quicken. That task was the responsibility of the public education system.

In the 1970s, however, a challenge was posed to the existing grid of what constituted those defining characteristics of American identity. Not that such challenges had not been put before. As early as the second decade of the century, men like Kallen and Bourne, already mentioned above, had been critical of an American culture which they saw as being over-dependent on an Anglocentric view of America's traditions (Trommler 1998). The mould into which all Americans were being assimilated was too restrictive: first, it denied non-English immigrants a sense of the worth of their backgrounds and origins and consequently burdened them with feelings of inferiority; and second, this process of assimilation unnecessarily limited the possibilities of cultural development by excluding the rich variety which was potentially available from other traditions. In the years which followed, these arguments were not entirely ignored. They certainly inspired later generations of critics who raised their voices against a perceived monoculturalism in the USA, and it is possible to see something of a shift from Anglocentric to Eurocentric views of the nation. In general terms, however, the upshot of these criticisms seems to have been simply to re-emphasize the diverse immigrant experience of the nation and the liberal ideology of the melting-pot metaphor without substantially changing the educational system, which remained oriented to an Anglo-Protestant version of American history and culture. It was the continuing dominance of this orientation which drew such virulent criticism from the 1970s onwards.

There seem to be four major charges laid against the existing educational programmes of that time. First, they misrepresented the nature of American society by ignoring the non-European origins of immigrants from Asia, Africa, and Central and South America. Second, they omitted the major contributions of individual non-Europeans to the development of the nation, contributions which should have been acknowledged both for their own sake and in order to provide role models for those children of non-European origin who were in danger of accepting the implicit social Darwinian model of racial inferiority on which the curriculum seemed to have been based. Third, the underachievement of non-European children could only be remedied by affirmative action, of a kind which would not only point to role models but also radically restructure the curriculum to take into account the very different cultural and social baggage which pupils brought to the classroom, so that substantive rather than token equality of opportunity was provided in the system. Fourth, a knowledge of the diversity of the world's historical and cultural traditions should be a requirement for all students in the interest of a greater understanding and tolerance, and in order to break through the parochialism which characterized American thinking and encouraged isolationism or – the new word – estrangement. The advocacy for radical change, predicated on a recognition both of the justice of these charges and the imperative need to address the problematic areas in the educational system to which they were related, has come to be labelled 'multiculturalism' in the USA.

Various proposals were put forward to bring about an overhaul of the system, ranging from programmes in bilingual education which would allow children from Hispanophone families to receive an education in Spanish, and thus eliminate the disadvantage they suffered in the classroom where the medium of instruction was different from their mother-tongue, to a rewriting of textbooks both to take account of the dark side of American history – the treatment of the slaves and the massacres of native Americans – and to highlight the achievements of non-whites and non-white civilizations that in both global and American history have made significant contributions to the development of mankind. These proposals were and are regarded by some conservatives as extremely radical and striking at the root of American identity, but they have also, for different reasons, been criticized by those on the left.

The conservative critics reject the multiculturalist proposals on various counts, but the underlying premise of their thinking is simply that the system has worked very well up to now and that it continues to work well under present circumstances. Any radical change would not merely fail to deal adequately with whatever social injustice may still exist; it would in fact exacerbate the situation, lead to greater injustice, bring about the fragmentation of the USA and generate the divisive anarchy which is so apparent in other areas of the world. As an example of misguided policy they point to bilingual education, which in their eyes perpetuates disadvantage (Schlesinger 1998: 112–16), since it prevents pupils from acquiring that mastery of English which is necessary for them to improve their status in society and to help them function efficiently in their dealings with the state. Far better to let them struggle in schools, so that eventually they can succeed in fully integrating themselves, if not in the second then at least in the third and subsequent generations. And as an example of the divisiveness which has already crept into the system they note the segregation of groups on university campuses into different associations with separate residential quarters for blacks, Hispanics, gays, Asians and Jews – a trend which they deplore.

Against this conservative backlash there have been two responses. The first has been to reiterate, with even more compelling and cogent examples, the earlier case of the injustice of the existing system, and, by such illustration, to pour scorn on the argument that the system is working relatively smoothly. Both by reference to sociological evidence backed up with statistics and by critical analysis of discourse, historical, cultural and political, they show how minority experience is undervalued and minorities kept at a perpetual disadvantage in relation to democratic participation in civil society. These two positions for and against are sufficiently familiar to us not to require any further description here, but before going on to consider the way in which the debate has been carried on by those who advocate multiculturalism but avoid the confrontational style of exchange described above, it is worth noting the different premise from which the arguments of conservatives and radicals begin, which perhaps explains the lack of mutual understanding and strong mutual antipathy of the two camps.

American liberalism has long been a champion of the rights of the individual, and it has regarded with horror the historical examples of totalitarian states which have curtailed those rights in the alleged interest of some greater common good. In the eyes of American liberalism – but rather than speak in abstractions let us say, in the minds of all Americans who have been thoroughly schooled by public institutions into a commitment to this principle – the state should not interfere with the freedom of individuals to express themselves in any way unless it can be conclusively shown that such self-expression impinges directly and critically on the lives and freedoms of others. The state, therefore, rather than seek to impose restrictions on citizens, should have as its *raison d'être* the facilitation of conditions which allow maximum freedom of individual expression. Any proposal for legislation which threatens the freedom of the individual is consequently resisted tooth and nail on the strength of the argument that it is an attack on the core notion of American identity. It is this type of reasoning which, for example, we see being wheeled in by the gun lobby in the USA: even though there have been abuses of the right to carry arms, it is preferable to tolerate the occasional abuse than to curtail the rights of the individual.

Running counter to this liberal position is the argument – and let us here not confine our discussion to the USA but broaden it out more generally – that in order to create the conditions in which all individuals have equality of opportunity with respect to the freedom of expression and the freedom to develop to the maximum their talents and abilities, it is necessary to make special provision for those who under the present circumstances labour under a dis-advantage: thus, for example, it is the state's responsibility to have in place a system of social welfare to cater for the mentally and physically disabled. Taking this one step further and putting the proposal in terms which appear more radical and hence potentially confrontational, it is necessary to empower those groups whose members, simply because of their group membership, are currently disempowered. Seeing the debate in these terms, one can quickly understand how the debate might and does develop into differen-tial assessments and evaluations of how disadvantaged and disem-powered specific groups are, and whether, even conceding group disadvantage, the correct remedy is to privilege groups rather than, in conformity with liberal principles, to target individuals, and maximize their chances. On the one side there is the old argument that the poor are responsible for their own plight, since the oppor-tunities for self-improvement are in place and they simply do not take advantage of them because of their own laziness and incom-petence. On the other is the argument that the poor are trapped in a cycle of poverty which cannot be broken unless, through state legislation, there is a massive transfer of wealth from the rich to the poor. So far as the specific debate on multiculturalism is concerned, the relevant arguments are that in the present system minorities need to be empowered through affirmative action which will take the form of, for example, quota places in higher education or employment legislation, even if this is at the expense of the domi-nant majority group.[1]

The criticism brought against such proposals is that they cause injustice to individuals from the majority group, since, in higher edu-cation for example, they are not competing for institutional places on an equal basis with those from minorities. A second point some-times made here is that affirmative action also creates a victim men-tality or feeling of inherent inferiority among individuals and groups, if they are made to think that they are constantly in need of special provisions to reach positions of high social status. By coinci-dence, on the day I write this, a letter has appeared in *The Guardian* newspaper making this same point, on this occasion in response to an article in the previous day's issue which had reported that a group of black writers and academics called for the removal of Tennyson's poems from the school syllabus, as 'not representative of today's young people'. Christopher Rollason writes in response:

> The cause of multiculturalism is best served by promoting non-Wasp writers not on ideological grounds but on their merits. Today's remarkable crop of Indian writers – Vikram Chandra, Amitav Ghosh, Anita Desai and others – have won recognition not through affirmative action quotas, but by drawing on eastern and western narrative traditions to create a new synthesis. That and not kneejerk obeisance to PC clichés, is the way forward for minority literatures.
>
> (*The Guardian*, 12 August 1999)

This is not the place to pursue these arguments, but it is well to have them in mind and to note how the debate turns upon a dichotomy between the group and the individual which, false as it may be, remains entrenched in current popular political thinking and has a pervasive influence on debates in the USA in particular.

Returning to the question of how we should assess the arguments about the relative advantages and disadvantages to a nation's citizens of a strategy of multiculturalism in education, we may find it helpful to employ here a distinction which is frequently made between so-called 'soft' multiculturalism and 'critical' multiculturalism. The first, with some reservations, has won some endorsement from the conservative lobby but hostility from the radicals, while the second is rejected by conservatives but has support from radical intellectuals. Soft multiculturalism, widely practised now in British schools, takes as its starting point the acknowledgement that the school curriculum needs to be revised in order to incorporate the experience of all pupils into the delivery of the syllabus of school subjects. In educational circles it is widely associated with the Swann Report, *Education for All*, commissioned by the government and published in 1985 (Rex 1996: 36–9; Grillo 1998: 179–81). Swann argued that the culture of the family and the domestic everyday routines of children need to be recognized with respect to everything ranging from religion to cuisine. By showing such an awareness of the family backgrounds of children, schools can make good pedagogical use of material which will facilitate learning, since such material draws immediately on what is familiar to children and leads them on from there, thus a positive learning environment is created to which children become more responsive. Through this public institutional recognition, cultural practices which pupils might have considered private to them and a source of differentiation from others, and in some cases a cause for embarrassment, are now transformed into acceptable customs and habits and a potential cause for pride. Their experience is thus valorized. This extension of examples beyond the normal range of pupils from the dominant majority culture educates the majority and helps to dispel the ignorance and prejudice which are so often the factors underlying discrimination and injustice inside and outside the school.

In order for these new initiatives to be successful there have to be carefully planned revisions of textbooks across the curriculum which will ensure that negative representations of other cultures are removed and that a judicious mix of references reflects the multicultural nature of contemporary society. More importantly, however, teachers need to be retrained to be able to administer the new syllabuses appropriately. This means overcoming an initial hostility to what is regarded as an unnecessary deviation from their previous good practice. It also means training in cultural awareness – taking care over unfamiliar non-European names, being sensitive to major non-Christian festivals – and encouraging a much greater openness to and intellectual curiosity in other cultures.

While these initiatives have been broadly welcomed they have, after the initial wave of enthusiasm, attracted some criticism (see Brah 1996: 227–34; Rex 1996: 178–80; Grillo 1998: 180–1; see also Asad 1993: 260–2). Some of this has come from staunch defenders of the Anglo-Protestant tradition who maintain that Britain is a Christian nation with a specific history and traditions and that the new multicultural emphasis seeks to deny this. It is this lobby which ensured that school assemblies should be predominantly Christian, something which raises eyebrows across the Channel in France where the school is considered a strictly secular institution. The major criticism has, however, come from those who argue that the initiatives undertaken in schools are mere tokenism (Grillo 1998: 194–203) and that, however well intentioned they may be, they do not get to grips with the real issues of overcoming institutionalized disadvantage and structural change. For such critics, although the new initiatives have raised awareness of the presence of ethnic minorities in Britain, the way in which they have done so is in effect by exoticizing them and hence perpetuating stereotypes of difference and, *ipso facto*, inferiority. The phrase frequently used to describe this exoticization is 'steel-bands, saris and samosas', picking up on three of the colourful signifiers of ethnic otherness. It is, claim the critics, these visible and tangible phenomena which are seized upon time and time again in schools as markers of cultural identity, and by failing to explore the deeper realities of ethnic minority experience schools trivialize other cultures, rendering them entertaining but superficial and peripheral. This reduction of ethnic minorities to a limited set of cultural traits is subsequently further endorsed by the media and becomes firmly ensconced in the national mentality, to the point where knowledge of the other is confined to dismissive referential images: Asians as Muslim fanatics or corner-shop owners; blacks as trouble-makers; Irish as drinkers, Chinese as pidgin-English speaking owners of takeaways. The success in Britain of the satirical television programme *Goodness Gracious Me!* – the phrase itself a mocking reference to Indian English – in which young Asian-British actors expose the absurdity of the majority image of what constitutes ethnic minority culture, is a reflection of how deeply embedded these notions are within public consciousness.

Satire is, of course, a very effective way of drawing attention to some of the problems – although there is always a risk that for some of the audience it will simply confirm their views.[2] However, say the critics, more must be done within schools not simply to dispel ignorance but to tackle the real disadvantages from which some ethnic minorities still suffer. To achieve this a much more thoroughgoing attempt to bridge the division between home and school is required by, for example, more concerted attempts to bring parents into the task of education, by a greater involvement of teachers in the understanding of minority experience, not simply tokenism, and by providing some education in the language medium of the home. At a more general level, it requires a radical examination of the way in which the present system is predicated on assumptions of white cultural and intellectual supremacy as reflected both consciously and unconsciously in styles of teaching, teaching materials themselves and, most damagingly, in the labelling of children on the basis of their ethnic background. Radical as these proposals may appear to be, especially to those who see them as undermining what they regard as a British way of life, one should recall that, *mutatis mutandis*, it is precisely this sort of restructuring and radical reorganization which has taken place in the education system as a

whole to take account of the recognition that the earlier system was
biased in favour of the middle classes. Taken in such a comparative
context, the protests of those who argue that the system is being
unduly loaded towards ethnic minorities resemble those of parents
of public school pupils who feel their sons are being unfairly
excluded from Oxford and Cambridge because of a bias in favour
of state schools.

That political correctness can lead to extreme proposals which
make easy targets for a conservative backlash is undeniable, but
those who argue for a stronger approach to multiculturalism than
the kind of tokenism which soft multiculturalism suggests maintain
that there are sound moral and intellectual grounds for adopting an
approach which they refer to as critical multiculturalism. The
purpose of critical multiculturalism, as usefully defined by Terence
Turner (1994: 408), is 'to use cultural diversity as a basis for challenging, revising and relativizing basic notions and principles
common to dominant and minority cultures alike, so as to construct
a more vital, open, and democratic common culture'. This type of
multiculturalism must be immediately distinguished from what
Turner calls difference multiculturalism, similar to what I have
referred to above as soft multiculturalism, and to what other radical
critics call corporate multiculturalism, which they describe as
employing a 'Benetton effect', namely the exploitation of ethnic
difference to promote commercial ends (Goldberg 1994: 8). The
principal drawback of difference multiculturalism lies in its essentializing of difference to the point where that alone is celebrated
and becomes a political goal in its own right rather than, as in the
case of critical multiculturalism, leading to an ongoing critical
engagement with both dominant and minority cultural experience.
For critical multiculturalists the revision of the curricula is a
welcome starting point, and the discussion of, for example, a new
textbook of American studies such as the *Heath*, which seeks radically to revise the canon (Bak 1993), is a welcome move, since the
health of a cultural tradition depends entirely on constant challenge, argument and revision, the essential preconditions of a
democratic culture.

Given the large aims of critical multiculturalism, its advocates
recognize that although the school is one of the sites in which critical ideas need to be explored it is only one of several such sites, and
that there are inherent problems in over-emphasizing education.
One difficulty is that already mentioned, of multiculturalism being

simply diluted into an easy celebration of difference. Another arises when multiculturalism joins up with cultural studies to foster exactly that critical engagement with everyday experience which is desired, but then finds itself the object of hostile criticism from those who see such criticism as politically partisan and accuse multiculturalists of political indoctrination. It is precisely at this point that the media and the liberal establishment raise their voices most stridently against what they perceive as the the dogma of political correctness and the evil of identity politics.

The arguments appear again to have come full circle. Critical multiculturalists (Chicago Cultural Studies Group 1994) respond to liberal criticism by distancing themselves from difference multiculturalists and denying any intention to substitute one dogma with another, to put in place polyethnic difference where once there was only Eurocentric uniformity. They argue that their purpose is to construct an environment of critical engagement which will involve an examination of traditions rather than an undermining of them, but hostile critics, aided by the media, are sceptical of such arguments and respond by pointing to examples of practice which in terms of their discourse appear absurd.

One interesting argument put forward to explain the level of popular antagonism towards multiculturalism and political correctness takes up this issue of discourse and suggests that the problems of misunderstanding and miscommunication which occur are a product of the discontinuity between academic debate and popular perceptions. Where continuity does exist is between the vocabulary and terms of reference of the humanities, history and English, which feed directly into the media and indeed constitute the terms of reference of the media itself. Inevitably, the debates on multiculturalism then take the form of discussions on that territory familiar to journalists and liberal intellectuals whose view of culture has been determined by their own grounding within a tradition of the humanities. In addition, they are writing and presenting programmes for those audiences which have equally been inducted into that tradition by both formal and informal education. Trying to insert social science concepts, especially those deriving from a discipline such as anthropology, knowledge of which remains largely confined to academic circles, at best risks confusion, and frequently leads to charges of jargon, obscurantism and wilful obfuscation.

There seems to me a great deal of truth in this argument of the discontinuity of discourse, which applies to British experience as much as to American. The strong appeal made to common sense as the ultimate arbiter, for example, seems predicated on just this sort of rhetorical divide. One remembers Thatcher's 'There is no such thing as society; there are only individuals', an expression representing not only her own sentiments but also, one suspects, those of many of her advisers and civil servants, simply unaccustomed to social science concepts and highly suspicious of sociology and anthropology as well as, a fortiori, of cultural studies. Seen from this perspective, the problem of how to win recognition for multiculturalism is not so much one of achieving a consensus on the merit of its objectives – who would argue with the goal of creating an environment in which a democratic culture can flourish? – as one of presentation: how to get across notions of justice, civil rights and empowerment of minorities to a public accustomed to a humanities-based discourse of individual freedom, and notions of a cultural tradition bounded by canons of moral value and aesthetic taste which appear to be universal and immutable.

For a variety of contingent historical reasons the most heated debates in which academics, intellectuals and the media in the USA have participated relate to the curriculum in education. The definition of a canon has always been significantly more important in the USA than in Britain. In accommodating the influx of immigrants of different origins and from different religious traditions there has been on the whole very little difficulty about tolerating non-Anglo-Protestant religious ritual – a different matter from allowing deviation from Anglo-Protestant culture in general which, as we have seen, has been the melting-pot to which all were urged to assimilate. The variety of Christian sects, the strong visibility of Jewish practice and the proliferation of cults and new age religions testify, if not to a fraternization between communities, at least to a reasonable degree of tolerance – indeed, this tolerance of religion is one of the fundamental promises of the Constitution (Ostendorf 1998: 51).[3] The practice of religious ritual in no way threatens the unity of the nation; the latter is assured by the continual recruitment of the young into an understanding of and commitment to what constitutes the American way of life, as articulated through the secular rituals of the state and in schools in particular. Sets of textbooks inculcate a definitive idea of what constitute American values, American history and American literature and culture. Not surprisingly, then, when these definitions are challenged it is in the arena of education that the fiercest debates take place. By contrast, in Britain the idea of a fixed canon is relatively recent; there have never been textbooks along the lines of the American model, and, at least until the Thatcher years, there was very little in terms of a nationally known version of British history. (There were of course popular references which everyone might recognize at least in outline, although even they may have been more familiar in parodic versions rather than in knowledge of the substance of the historical events.) Consequently, with so much less national capital invested in canonical tradition, and indeed with resistance to the very idea of canon formation – note the hostility to Leavis' notorious work *The Great Tradition*, which sought to impose by fiat a dogma of literary evaluation – the discussion in educational circles about the composition of syllabuses has attracted relatively little attention. Occasionally conservative eyebrows are raised at the inclusion of Caribbean writers into a school syllabus aimed at 16–18-year-olds, and with boring regularity one encounters public discussions about standard English and its advantages and disadvantages to those from cultural and economic minorities, but on the whole these debates, even when they do surface in the popular media, do not stir the passions as they do in the USA. In Britain, on the contrary, it is religious belief and ritual as commented on by the media which lead to the angriest exchanges.

The best-known recent instance of such angry religious debates in Britain surrounded the publication of Salman Rushdie's book, *The Satanic Verses*. A large number of Muslims felt offended by the book because it appeared to ridicule their religion through satire and caricature, and because of what they regarded as blasphemous references to God and insulting remarks about the Prophet Muhammad. The initial disquiet among some members of the Muslim community in Britain was fanned into a flame by the edict of Ayatollah Khomeini condemning to death Salman Rushdie for what he had written.

The non-Muslim British, relying on their media, were taken aback by the strength of the Muslim protest and there ensued an acrimonious exchange of opinions which filled correspondence columns in the newspapers for some weeks[4] and gave rise to what is still an ongoing debate about the limits of religious freedom in a liberal society. Before examining what precisely both sides regard as being at stake in this debate, a word is called for on why the issue raised such passions. In particular, we need to understand why the non-Muslim British public was so shaken by the stance of most Muslims, including those on what might be termed the open-liberal wing of the religion.

In European societies, particularly those of northern Europe, there has been since the middle of the eighteenth century a rapid move to the secularization of civil society. This has taken different forms and has been frequently commented on by social scientists and theologians who have used terms such as 'disenchantment' (Max Weber) and 'demythologizing' (Bultmann) to describe this process. In effect, the result of this historical trend, sometimes referred to as the Enlightenment project, has been to restrict more and more the areas of public life which are regarded as the concern of religion.[5] Hand in hand with this secularization has gone a movement in art and literature which, while regarding the issues of morality and reason raised in an earlier age by religion as of fundamental importance, sees the best way to encourage debate and reflection as lying in the demystification of religious symbols and personalities. Only through iconoclasm can the necessary breakthrough be made to rational thinking unfettered by superstition. Consequently, in northern Europe, and especially in former communist countries, ridiculing Christian figures, mocking superstition and undermining the cult of personality associated with both saints and living priests have become an accepted element of the contemporary European cultural heritage, which followers of the religion may well not like but which they are prepared to live with and engage against in open debate.

One factor which has facilitated this tolerance of attacks on religion appears to have been a theological tradition in Christianity which has over the centuries permitted the anthropomorphizing of God and the pictorial representation of Christ. Subsequent theological debate has then been about the accuracy of these accounts and representations of God. Within the Muslim world, however, it is, and has been since the beginnings of the religion, the very act of representation itself which is regarded as sacrilegious, irrespective of whether the representation is good or bad. In Muslim scriptures there is a strong injunction against the anthropomorphizing of God so that even the ascription of a gender to God, something which is common within Christianity, is regarded as blasphemous. Nor is it in any way permissible to draw or paint or make figures representing the Prophet. (It was precisely because this was so well understood that the makers of the film *The Message*, which showed the origins of Islam, studiously avoided any direct portrayal of the Prophet.) Given this enduring and strictly obeyed prohibition on representation, the anger of Muslims at an account which not only represented the never-to-be-represented but caricatured the religion into the bargain, becomes more understandable; and given the ordinariness of representation in Christianity and the ignorance of non-Muslim British about Islam we can now understand why the arguments became so heated. Although ostensibly the disagreement turned on the publication of *The Satanic Verses*, both sides were talking past each other. Non-Muslims regarded the issue as one of freedom of speech, democracy and resisting the tyranny of what they regarded as unacceptable religious obscurantism; Muslims saw it as an occasion on which it was imperative to put into the domain of public discourse what was of such fundamental importance to them that they felt their sense of identity and integrity coming under attack. Unfortunately, but predictably given the way in which much of the media polarizes issues in the interests of sensationalism rather than uses such occasions for constructive debate, with only a few exceptions, it was the extremists whose views were given most airing.

One of the deplorable consequences of uninformed public debate about religion when it arises *ad hoc* as a consequence of a single issue is that it so quickly leads to people taking up intransigent positions. From here it is a short step to adopting a Manichaean vision of the world in which the other is only capable of being perceived as the enemy, all of whose actions must be scrutinized for the evil intent they contain. This of course applies not only to Muslim–Christian confrontations. In Britain one is only too well aware how much of the debate on Northern Ireland has led to this sort of embittered polarization. Still, there is cause for concern in the degree to which Muslims have become so demonized in Western eyes, replacing Communism in the opinion of political scientists like Samuel Huntingdon (1993), for example, as the greatest threat to world peace. Unless checked, this tendency to see the worst in the other can often escalate into violence – as has occurred against Muslim minorities in India and Christian minorities in Pakistan and recently against minorities of both religions in different localities in eastern Indonesia – and frequently leads to bitterness and hostility over relatively trivial incidents.

In France, where state education is strictly secular, any manifestation of religious belief is potentially vulnerable to criticism and disciplinary action. When Muslim girls wore veils and headscarves into the classroom they were told that this was unacceptable and a major public argument erupted, leading again to the characterization of Muslim demands as a potential threat to the secular principles of the French republic, but with others arguing that there was no prohibition on girls wearing crosses to school and that that practice had never been considered a threat to secularism. This controversy over headscarves created a worrying alliance between the right and some of those on the left, both hostile in this case to public expressions of Muslim faith.[6]

Similar confrontational issues have emerged in Europe in relation to the ritual slaughter of animals for food. Orthodox Muslims and Jews require that meat for consumption is taken only from animals which have been killed according to proper ritual practice, a requirement which involves cutting the throat of the living animal. In Britain this method of slaughter appears in violation of regulations which require animals to be killed by first stunning them and then shooting bolts into the brain, regarded by current legislation as being the most humane method of slaughter. This has now become a contentious matter, leading to the branding of orthodox Muslims and Jews as behaving in some way out of line with the moral majority (Alderman 1995).

Potentially a more divisive issue, and one in which the divisions cannot neatly be drawn between religious and non-religious opinion, concerns religious schools. Within Britain there have for some time been Christian schools which are state-supported. These are schools where the national curriculum is followed and where the pupils do national examinations. A substantial part of schools' activities is also given over to religious instruction and prayer, and the whole ethos of the school is religious. The support which the state indirectly gives to religion in this way has in the past been attacked by critics who want to see the same clear-cut distinctions made in education between, on the one hand, the public and the secular, and, on the other, the private and the religious, as can be found in the USA and France. On the whole, though, in Britain this has not been a subject of much public discussion, at least until recently. Now, however, as a result of demands for similar recognition for Jewish, Muslim and Sikh educational institutions, it has become a major factor in the debate about multiculturalism in Britain.

At first glance there would appear to be little room for disagreement, given the principle of state subsidies for Christian schools: if one religious denomination is entitled to such support then so too should others. However, there have been several arguments mounted against the extension of the range of state-aided religious schools. First, the lobby which has consistently opposed state-supported religious education of any denomination has pushed the case that with the pressure on the state to reduce support for religion, the expansion of the religious schools sector is a regressive step, since in essence it seems to create or reassert a natural bond between state and religion which should be severed once and for all: religion should be a private matter. Second, there are those who, while happy to see the continuing support of Christian schools, oppose the extension to other denominations because they regard the teachings of those other religious traditions as being in opposition to the democratic traditions of the nation. Hence the letters to the newspapers about not paying taxes to support the preaching of religious traditions which regard women as second-class citizens. Finally, there are those from within the community of the minority religions themselves who regard the segregation of religious groups from each other, which is the inevitable consequence of the creation of new religious schools, as leading to the break-up of a sense of British identity and a fragmentation of the nation into a kind of plural society in which there will be no common commitment to a set of national ideals but, instead, exclusivity and minimal tolerance.

For this latter group the pressure for the establishment of religious schools is fully understandable given the discrimination and abuse which pupils from religious minorities often face in mainstream state schools. Within the security of denominational schools pupils are protected from this abuse and consequently gain self-confidence and thrive in an educational environment where they and their religion are respected. However, argues Yasmin Alibhai-Brown, a well-known writer on multicultural matters in Britain, in the context of a comment on a Sikh school recently granted state support (*The Independent*, 2 December 1999), the social price which has to be paid is too high, since pupils grow up too little aware of other religious traditions, and the result of exclusivity is to reinforce and consolidate prejudice and separateness. The answer, in her opinion, must be to create a state system which is equitable to all, where minority status does not lead to abuse and discrimination but provides a space for the exploration of each other's traditions and a tolerance and openness which will allow for

the emergence of a truly multicultural society. Fine words, say her
opponents, but in the present climate, in the interests of this generation of children, the strategy must be one of campaigning for more
religious schools.

In reviewing these debates and others like them in Britain and
elsewhere on the relationship between the institutions of the state
and the religion of its citizens, we can distinguish three sets of arguments. The first concerns the degree to which the state is or should
be an instrument for the implementation of a set of principles
derived from religious belief. The Islamic ideal here is clear: there
can be no conceptual division between religious and other
domains; consequently politics, government and law in a Muslim
state must be informed by teachings in the Islamic tradition. There
can be no division between Caesar and God as there is in Christianity. In fact, there are radical Christians who would argue the
same about their Christian principles of morality and justice,
namely that they should inform every aspect of the state's actions.
However, the current consensus in Christian countries would
appear to hold strongly to a division between state and religion,
and argue that the major ideological movement of Western society
over the last two or three centuries has been to loosen the grip of
religion and replace it with the philosophy of liberal democracy.
Nevertheless, despite the pretensions of this argument to tran-
scend or supersede religion, there is a strong body of academic
opinion which regards the very argument itself as being thoroughly
imbued with Christianity-derived ideas and therefore fatally
flawed epistemologically: the argument that we must not allow
religion to influence the practice of government is seen to be itself
a Christian idea. Consequently, far from being a position tran-
scending religious difference, the liberal view is derived from
within a very specific religious tradition and therefore cannot be
used as a universal metaprinciple on which to challenge other
religious traditions which take a more supportive view of the
interpenetration of religion and social organization.

A second set of discussions, linked to but slightly different from
the above, turns on a formula which associates the state with the
public domain and religion with the private. Here the argument,
rather than taking a perspective which has an institutional focus, is
predicated on the rights of the individual and in particular the
freedom of religion. Seen from this point of view, religion, along
with freedom of speech, is one of the fundamental liberties which

the state should guarantee for the individual, that is, the state must ensure that the individual is allowed to exercise those liberties, not without any restriction or limits but at least to the point where they do not infringe the liberties of others. A corollary of this is that, as in the reference to God and Caesar above, a conceptual division is made between public and private domains. The state, under this view, need do nothing beyond guaranteeing the conditions which permit individuals to practise their religion in private. Try as they might to defend such a position, however, commentators have ultimately had to concede that this public–private dichotomy is as unworkable in relation to religion as it is in relation to expressions of ethnicity, and that one is constantly merging into the other to the point where they cannot be separated (Grillo 1998: 204).

The difficulties over demarcating public and private spheres, it should be noted, are not confined to areas of religion and ethnic identity. There is constant debate about the degree to which what happens within the domestic privacy of the house is regarded as lying within the public domain with respect, for example, to the rights of the child. (This concern for the welfare of the child can also, incidentally, have specific religious and ethnic dimensions when people campaign against the circumcision of baby boys, a religious duty among some groups, as being contrary to the rights of the child.)

The upshot of the abandoning of the dichotomy of public and private domains, as far as religious practice is concerned, is that there is now a general recognition that the state cannot be satisfied with the negative stance of simply confining religion to a private sphere, and that in order to guarantee religious freedom it must act positively to intervene where necessary and create conditions to allow a community of believers to fulfil the demands of their faith. One can see that in the first place this may mean making spaces available for the erection of places of public worship, and, for the most part and despite occasional local protests, this type of development is uncontroversial. Where disagreement and controversy do arise is when religious communities make additional demands such as requesting exemptions from statutory legislation on religious grounds – for example, Sikhs requesting the right to be allowed to wear their turbans and not being subject to safety-helmet regulations. The building of special abattoirs for ritual slaughter would also come under this class of demands;[7] as would the lobby for state-supported religious schools. With respect to issues like these in particular, religion can no longer remain a private affair and becomes a matter of general public concern.

In Britain, France and other European countries which have only in the last three or four decades seen a substantial rise in the population of non-Christian citizens, governments have often acted in an *ad hoc* fashion as issues have arisen – schoolgirls wearing veils, permissions to build temples, outlawing of female circumcision – but as yet there has been no concerted, systematic attempt to think through the moral and legal implications of the right to religious freedom. In other countries of the world the state has taken up a variety of positions. Where, for example, the national state comprises a number of different ethnic groups of different beliefs there is often a measure of tolerance and sometimes support for minority religions, or at least this used to be the case until relatively recently: I am thinking here of countries such as India and Indonesia where the official government position, enshrined in the constitutions of the state – an embattled one at present – is of support for minorities. In other countries where governments have been anti-religious, there has often been suppression – though, paradoxically, at just the time when countries which were formerly liberal are now becoming intolerant, many former communist countries are now seemingly more respectful of religious freedoms.

In effect, though, what immediately stands out when we examine issues of religious tolerance and intolerance throughout the world, whether we choose to look at government policies or the instances of religious conflict generated spontaneously, is a profound confusion between ethnicity and religion. It is this confusion which lies at the root of a third set of arguments about religion and the state and affects the perceptions of all parties to these debates.

Among religious believers, for example, what is often a local colouring of the religion is taken to be fundamental to the faith, that same colouring being regarded as idolatrous elsewhere. An example of this in Christianity would be the veneration of the saints in Mediterranean Europe as perceived by Protestants. This pluralism of ritual expression within religions frequently fails to be recognized, and this failure leads to tensions between majority and minority groups. The practice of keeping women in seclusion is, for example, frequently identified with Islam, rather than being identified as the cultural practice of a specific ethnic group which derives from non-Muslim traditions. Consequently, Islam is frequently portrayed as a religion which regards women as inferior; and this in turn leads to the stigmatization of the religion.

A more nuanced approach is to recognize that religion and ethnic affiliation are two separate things but that often a set of religious beliefs, like a common language and a common origin, can be regarded as a criterial feature of ethnic identity. This too, however, can lead to curious anomalies in legislation. In Britain, for example, there is legislation in place which outlaws discrimination on the basis of ethnicity. Thus it is illegal to refuse someone employment simply on the basis of their ethnic identity. If a set of religious beliefs is considered an essential component of the identity of that ethnic group and a refusal of employment can be shown to be linked to religious practice then this is in contravention of the law. However, if there is no integral connection between religious practice and ethnic identity, say in the case of an English convert to Islam, then the refusal to employ on religious grounds is not illegal (Faisal Bodi 1999). However, a recent attempt to rectify this anomaly by introducing legislation against discrimination on the grounds of religion ran into fierce controversy.[8]

These anomalies and the confusion over ethnic identity, minority rights and religious freedom plague discussion of multiculturalism throughout the world. One thing that emerges from the confusion is the difficulty of separating religious ideas and beliefs from a whole range of other issues relating to rights and civil liberties in general. Nor will it work, as we have seen, to confine some areas to a private domain and others to the public. Some more general framework will need to be worked out, one which ultimately goes beyond the narrow confines of a national ideology, be it the American creed or the British way of life. But it is precisely a fear of the more general and universal and the reluctance to abandon the national ideology which brings together in strange alliance commentators like Schlesinger and Alibhai-Brown. The latter attacks the recent establishment of a state-supported Sikh school because of its exclusivity. Implicitly she is sceptical about the claims of the school to be teaching a higher morality. She fears that the growing trend towards the proliferation of such schools will lead to children never learning what constitutes a British identity, and consequently there will be no set of common core national values which all will share. The result will be fragmentation and a loss of everything that she holds dear about British society. Religious exclusivism is therefore the enemy and state support for such schools should be resisted. This is an opinion widely held among liberals in Britain (and in France, as we have seen). Schlesinger identifies the same danger, the loss of a national tradition and heritage, in his case that of the USA, which is threatened not so much by religious lobbies as by the challenge being mounted to the curricula of schools and universities. Both Schlesinger and Alibhai-Brown (2000) recognize the vitality of other traditions and both recognize the importance of providing educational opportunities for learning about these other traditions, but both feel strongly that there is a specific national tradition and history to which all citizens should be committed.

From a multiculturalist perspective the problem with their concept of national traditions comes from a static and idealized view of national culture. Despite their protestations to the contrary – and Alibhai-Brown would be particularly voluble on this score – they take positions which essentialize culture, giving it the quality of a compartmentalized and separate way of acting and feeling which, though it may be influenced by ideas which permeate cultural boundaries, nevertheless remains essentially itself. This concept of a national culture is increasingly difficult to sustain when the highly visible process of global change gives ample confirmation to the arguments of social anthropologists that social forms and cultural traditions in all societies are constantly in a state of flux.[9] The idea of a specific national culture impervious to change is an illusion born of nineteenth-century European romanticism or, in other parts of the world, from various Asian conservative creeds such as neo-Confucianism, and we should not allow ourselves to be deceived by it.

Nevertheless, however much we may doubt the salience of categories and concepts such as a national culture and tradition, it remains true that there are large numbers of people for whom they are an unquestionable reality, and in debates on multiculturalism their views need to be taken into account. In pressing them to examine and define more closely what constitutes a national tradition and what they consider the place of religious and educational institutions within that tradition, we will be engaging in that necessary dialogue so vital for reaching a consensus not only within a national but also in a global community.

Notes

1 See the papers in Shapiro and Kymlicka (1997) for some excellent discussions on these issues in different national contexts.
2 See the controversy which broke out about the white comedian Ali G, whose taking on of a black persona caused offence to some (*The Guardian*, 12 January 2000). A video of the interviews conducted by Ali G was produced at the end of 1999 by Channel 4 entitled *Ali G innit.*
3 See also the remarks of Hall and Lindholm (1999: 24–5) on the tolerance of religious pluralism in the USA as partly arising from the influence of the Virginian plantocracy's indifference to the diversity of Christian sects to be found in the early USA.
4 Asad (1993: 269–306) gives an excellent account of how we should interpret these 'readings' of Rushdie's book.
5 Casanova (1994) has written a penetrating comment on this process and its contemporary significance, to which Asad (1999) has responded.
6 See Silverman (1992: 111–18) for a well-balanced account of the positions taken by intellectuals on different sides of the debate at the time, and see Hargreaves (1995: 125–31) for a chronology of the affair and a discussion of the legal principles associated with *laïcité* (secularism) in schools.
7 See 'Des élus marseillais dénoncent l'absence de mosquée et de lieu d'abattage rituel', *Le Monde*, 26 November 1999.
8 See the article by Polly Toynbee in *The Guardian*, 29 October 1999, and the correspondence which followed.
9 See similar remarks by Parekh (1995: 268) on the nature of national identity.

Cultural Diversity and Global Uniformity

In a recent article, David Crystal (1999) drew attention to the alarming rate at which languages are disappearing. The disappearance of languages is not a new phenomenon, he said; what is new is the rapidity with which it is now occurring. Of the world's estimated 6000 languages, 3000 would be gone in the next 50 years as the last speakers of those languages died. He gave several reasons why this was happening, but perhaps foremost among them was the inability of minority languages to compete in the contemporary world with the strength of dominant languages. He described a familiar pattern where groups which come into direct contact with dominant languages through movement to the cities and through the nation-wide promotion of a national language become familiar with those languages. In the second generation they have bilingual skills, but that bilingualism dies out in subsequent generations when the original native language of a group or a family is considered a source of embarrassment. As a result of this process happening now on a global scale linguistic diversity is diminishing. This disturbing trend requires our immediate attention, says Crystal, and we should do our best to protect and safeguard endangered languages.

The same argument is frequently made at a broader level about cultures, taken here again to be the distinctive ways of life of ethnic groups or, stretching it a bit, of nations. These too, it is claimed, are fast disappearing as a consequence of globalization. Multiculturalism in terms of diversity and difference appears, then, to be under threat from global convergence. The clearest evidence of such globalization comes from the changes in consumption patterns throughout the world. The ubiquitous Coca-Cola and McDonald's are the best-known examples of this trend. Those who regard this phenomenon positively argue that there is a clear demand for these products and that to deny consumers access to them is not just to hinder the development of free-market capitalism but to adopt an unacceptably paternalist and repressive attitude to consumers. That indeed there is a high demand for such products, they go on to say, can be seen on any day in the shopping malls of such major cities as Kuala Lumpur, Singapore, Bangkok and Jakarta, where crowds of people all coveting prestigious foreign brand names wander around shops crammed largely with imported items from shirts and handbags to watches and perfumes.[1] If, then, there is such a demand then why not let people decide for themselves whether they desire these goods and whether they wish to purchase them?

Their opponents sometimes regard this *laissez-faire* attitude with a horror springing from a dislike of global capitalism in general; more often, they accept capitalist principles yet deplore the lack of checks and controls on the excesses of the system. In their view the advocates of the free market fail to perceive the manner in which there is, despite appearances, only limited freedom of operation for countries of the South, the developing world, which are forced into accepting world trade agreements which are disadvantageous to them. Furthermore, consumers within these countries are subject to overwhelming advertising and marketing pressures the dimensions of which they are unaware of, and hence their choices and preferences are being determined for them. An example of the way in which such pressures are exercised lies in the domination of the global entertainment industry by the distribution of products from the USA, Europe and Australia. So in thrall are viewers to the images and consumer values implicit and explicit in programmes – very often largely confined to action films and soaps – that they seek to emulate lifestyles of these significant virtual others, and the market, having artificially created the demand, provides them with the opportunity to gratify those desires in the market-place. The upshot of these global trends is the death of local creativity and locally specific goods and their replacement by products reflecting Western cultural preferences.

At another level there is a greater fear that these changes in patterns of consumption represent even greater changes in the outlook and attitudes of people. Thus along with changes in what people prefer to eat and wear there comes a change in moral values and in the quality of the relationship between people. With increasing pressure to obtain the means for oneself to be able to live the desired new lifestyle comes a diminishing interest in taking responsibility for others. Putting it crudely, there is a fear of a shift from the community- and family-centred values of countries of the South to the individualist ethic of the consumerist North.

Such criticisms, however, fail to impress the supporters of globalization, who see them as unrealistically sentimental in their assumption of a simplistic dichotomy between harmonious communal traditions on the one hand and strife-ridden individualism on the other. They are particularly suspicious when the criticisms are voiced by politicians laying claim, for example, to a concept of Asian values which they are intent against preserving against the encroachments of the Western world. Very often the arguments of the politicians seem designed for little purpose other than to justify the curbs on democratic freedoms which they impose. The entertainment industry and global media in general, then, may be encouraging a uniformity of desire, but it should be remembered that the desire in question extends far beyond simple consumerism to demands for greater freedom of expression, accountability of the government and, most importantly, civil liberties in general. Thus the decline of local industry must be set against not just the long-term future and economic prosperity of a more efficient system of global production but also the immediate gains of an increasing general consciousness of justifiable rights and expectations. To reduce arguments about globalization to a discussion of consumerism, then, is to fail to understand the complexity of a situation in which at the same time as there occurs a transfer in patterns of consumption there is also taking place a shift in perceptions which is empowering large numbers of people in the world.

On the other hand, to assume that greater availability of the international communications media will lead to rapid changes in the restructuring of society to the advantage of those who are currently dispossessed is equally naive. Creating a demand for Dunkin' Donuts and Levi's 501s is very different from creating the conditions for a participatory democracy, and it is by no means certain that the one necessarily entails the other or that there are solid grounds for optimism.[2] Furthermore, it is at least superficially the case that modernization seems to have led throughout the world to a decline in those characteristic features of cultures by which the identity of ethnic groups is most immediately recognized. We have already noted the decline in minority languages. The same observation could also have been made about styles of dress or, at perhaps a more significant level, artistic and cultural performances. Take the Javanese shadow play, for example. It has long been recognized as perhaps the most distinctive single feature which represents and reproduces Javanese culture in its most condensed symbolic form. The stories of the Hindu-Javanese epics of the *Mahabharata* and *Ramayana* which are the subject of the plays, and the overall social and cultural context in which performances are held, have frequently been the subject of commentaries which demonstrate how the shadow play theatre and its cast of characters epitomize the moral values, aesthetic preferences and indeed the whole *Weltanschauung* of the Javanese. It is through the actions and attitudes portrayed in the world of the shadow plays that one comes to an understanding of what the Javanese hold dear and how they view the world. Yet, central as it is, performances of these plays are now much less frequent than they used to be. Only occasionally will rich patrons arrange for a full performance lasting into the early hours of the morning to celebrate some important family event, a wedding or a circumcision or an important anniversary. Instead, tourists are treated to one-hour performance snippets held in international hotels. True, knowledge of the universe of wayang figures is still widespread through the community, but there are now other heroes and heroines, of American, Japanese and Chinese origin, to compete with the exemplary role models of the wayang.

This type of cultural loss is not, of course, confined to countries of the developing world where 'culture contact' and postcolonialism seem to spell the death of indigenous traditions. In northern Europe there has been a noticeable loss of 'traditional' ways of life, some the result of major structural changes in the economy which have led to the loss of a particular industry, fishing or coal-mining for example, and with it the loss of that community's culture; in other cases, mechanization has brought with it the decline of specialist crafts and skills; and in the sphere of entertainment, reliance on television has led to a decline of community pastimes. Increased mobility, too, has meant that people no longer expect to stay rooted to the same neighbourhood, and the search for employment and experience now takes people away from their home and into new environments. Thus a sense of community and, with it, a sense of distinctive culture are lost.

These references to the decline of community in Europe, couched as they are in a frame of nostalgic reverie for the past, should, however, give us pause. How precisely should we evaluate the nature of the changes which have taken place in Europe and are taking place in similar forms elsewhere? Two connected views have a direct bearing on this question. The first, most clearly articulated in Williams (1973), warns us to beware of the romantic conservatism which looks back fondly to a past, only recently disappeared, in which the quality of life appears to have been so much better. Williams points out that this theme of an idealized past from which the present has degenerated is a constant trope in English literature, where the traditions of the village community were forever being described as having just passed away. The village in fact was never as it was imagined to be and present constructions of the community's past must always be interpreted as statements, often of a political nature, about the present. Extending Williams's argument beyond the nation, one can see that this same tendency to romanticize the past in the interests of justifying our criticisms of the present has also affected our perceptions of cultures other than our own. In this respect scholars have shown that the paradigmatic accounts of the modernization of Western society written by people such as Ferdinand Tönnies, describing the movement from *Gemeinschaft* to *Gesellschaft* and regretting the loss of the village community, were then transposed on to the colonies in the late nineteenth and early twentieth centuries. There, administrators and ethnographers used the same typologies and dichotomies to describe the colonial situation, and again in their perceptions the break-up of the wholesomeness of a native tradition was attributable to the modernization of the colony which was bringing in its wake disastrous consequences for local populations. As subsequent scholarship has shown, however, the village in the East, no more than in Europe, has never been the Arcadian community that romantic imagination would have it.

This first perspective on the nature of social change and corresponding cultural loss, developed especially by historians and literary critics, then, both questions the historical accuracy of the accounts which describe and attribute change to the recent past and at the same time raises doubts about the categories which are being used in the debates. What are these traditions which are disappearing? What elevates them as ways of behaving which are quasi-sacrosanct? When does transformation become disappearance? This is not to deny that some cultural loss of a kind is occurring. We know that languages have died out; similarly, we know that technical and artistic skills and knowledges disappear, but then the task must be to record the knowledge while it still exists so that it is there available in the archive, rather than to lament change and try to hang grimly on to decontextualized intellectual artefacts.

The second view, while again challenging the received historical record, takes the argument in a different direction. First, in relation to the effects of colonialism and its allegedly homogenizing influence, critics have recently argued that the description of colonized peoples simply submitting to the colonial powers and surrendering to the political, economic and educational institutions imposed on them neglects the strong resistance mounted against such impositions and fails to see the way in which the whole process of colonialism was at various points subverted and undermined. In short, it wrongly ascribes passivity rather than agency to peoples and communities who were actively engaged in determining their response to changing social and economic circumstances. In order to correct this misrepresentation of the colonial cultural encounter which has come down to us, scholars have consequently focused on those historical situations which had previously escaped the notice of those intent on constructing a narrative which would demonstrate the inexorable demise of local institutions.

This approach, with its focus on moments of resistance, has become most closely associated with the subaltern studies school, originally set up by a group of Indian social scientists and historians who, taking their inspiration from Gramsci, have regularly published sets of essays entitled *Subaltern Studies* (Guha 1982). Through a series of micro-historical cases they have demonstrated the significance in the colonial context of the notion of agency. Subsequently, this interpretive schema has been adopted in reappraising the histories of other regions of the world and has proved especially fruitful in the review of processes of transformation in peasant societies. In particular, it has provided a useful corrective to those 'world-systems' accounts which stressed to the exclusion of other features the economic incorporation of the peasantries into global markets. In fact, however, despite the vigorous polemics between the two sides to this debate, there seems to me to be less space between them than perhaps they would both admit. That the peasantries and horticultural cultivators of the world have over centuries, indeed millennia, been producing for global markets is not something which is any longer open to argument, but that production of this kind turned them into passive instruments of mercantilism and then capitalism simply does not reflect the complexity of the local response to what were regarded as welcome opportunities as much as, or even more often than, burdensome impositions. Moreover, as far as the diversity of cultures is concerned, the process of political and social change consequent on the successive economic developments which were occurring led to a constant evolution of cultural forms. In a historical perspective these forms are inherently unstable, ever subject to exogenous and endogenous influences and therefore always undergoing modification and transformation. And this would hold true not only with respect to political and economic institutions governing the modes of production within a particular society, but also with respect to artistic and cultural performance, religious ritual and the values and moral orientations of that society. In this perspective culture is neither a fixed set of social practices autonomously isolable from the currents of history, nor a simple reflection or index of political and economic change.[3]

The concept of continuous evolution thus needs to be borne constantly in mind, and for me is vividly evoked by a pithy Malay saying. The people of Sumatra have always held very strongly to the notion of an evolving tradition and have never been tempted to objectify their cultural practice. The word *adat* for them signifies the whole range of institutions from law and politics to performance, ritual and everyday behaviour. As they express it, *kain dipakai usang, adat dipakai baru* ('make constant use of your cloths and they are eventually worn thin, make constant use of *adat* and it is eternally renewed').

We owe a further point about the openness of tradition to innovation to contributions made by feminist scholarship which has significantly enlarged our understanding of cultural change. The earlier narratives, whether they celebrated the inexorability of the ultimate triumph of Enlightenment liberalism or regretted the passing of traditional society, both tended to render partial and simplistic accounts of local institutions since they ignored the dimension of gender. Any reviewing of cultural transformations in the future, therefore, in addition to being predicated on a concept of the continuous evolution of cultural forms, must develop a sensitivity to the gender dimension in order to avoid the grave structural flaws of earlier accounts. Consequently, whether the descriptions relate to the effects of the commoditization of agricultural production in developing countries or the sociology of kabuki theatre in the Edo period in Japan, scholars need to be alert to the gender dynamics of what was and is happening, not simply because this adds a further shade to the descriptive account but because it is central to any understanding of the logic of cultural development.

Further extensions to these arguments on the significance of agency pose other radical challenges to the way in which we should evaluate concepts such as globalization, with its suggestion of the loss of cultural diversity. Anthropologists, for example, whose privileged position in constantly crossing cultural and national boundaries has made them especially alert to signifiers of cultural identity, have commented on the highly individualistic way in which the products of global capitalism have been consumed at a local level. This observation draws our attention away from the product itself – whether it is a McDonald's hamburger or a blueprint for a style of corporate managerial practice – and directs our gaze to local practice and the significance of the item according to local cultural perceptions, a timely reminder that we should not assume that because the same item is to be found widely available in different countries, it plays a similar role in the construction of social reality (Appadurai 1986; Hannerz 1992). Thus, to return to our observation of the popularity of Western fast food franchises in Southeast Asia, we need to contextualize our perception by noting, for example, the greater frequency with which people in the region eat out, the occasions on which fast food is preferred to other cuisines, whether it is regarded as supplementary to the main diet, who, sociologically, the consumers are, and the intentions or semiological statements underlying this form of consumption. We also need to conduct longitudinal studies over time rather than be seduced by immediate reactions to novelty products. Taking these and other such issues into account, we might be less inclined to move to a conclusion of the homogenizing influence of global capitalism, and more disposed to regard the greater global availability of consumer items as adding to the general cultural repertoire rather than detracting from it.

An obvious and telling example of the processes of the transformation of the cultural significance of an institution would be the global dissemination of Christmas. Seen from one perspective, this phenomenon would appear to confirm the worst fears of those

critics of globalization who see in it nothing but the cynical exploitation of a commercial opportunity by the agents of global capitalism, stoking demand to create profits for themselves in a way which
is socially irresponsible and culturally destructive. Anthropologists,
however, have pointed out the way in which Christmas celebrations
simply add another dimension to the cultural life of communities
(Miller 1993). Putting up decorations and sending Christmas cards
does not mean the displacement of other secular rituals, far less
does it mean the abandonment of one religious tradition for
another. Descriptions of Sikh celebrations in London show how
this adoption of Christmas symbols provides additional cultural
opportunities for a community. Furthermore, they bring confirmation of a long-held anthropological truism that the same symbolic
objects carry different semantic weight both between groups and
communities and even among individuals within a community, and
this difference affects and is affected by practice. Among Sikhs in
Southall, for example, the children's birthday party, a relatively
new phenomenon, is taken as an opportunity for relatives of the
children to get together in concelebration rather than as among the
white population where the occasion is usually one from which all
adults, apart from the hosts, are only too glad to be absent
(Baumann 1992).

This example shows, then, how a relatively recently established
set of Western practices around Christmas – Christmas cards,
one recalls, were an invention of the nineteenth century – can be
taken on by communities among whom the rituals were formerly
unknown. (An instant confirmation of this comes from a news item
on the radio informing me that the Chinese are about to establish
a Christmas theme park near Beijing in the near future.) We might,
however, reasonably draw the conclusion from these examples that
yes, diversity and access to that diversity are growing but this is
fundamentally a one-way process of the export of cultural and
material products from the developed to the developing nations of
the world, dominant cultures pushing out weak ones, even though,
in the process, the shape of the cultural item and its significance
change. At one level this perception is easily countered by
reference, for example, to the spread of international cuisines.
McDonald's may be ubiquitous, but apparently chicken tikka
masala is the most popular dish in Britain; and the evidence of
Chinese takeaways, Middle Eastern kebab houses and the widespread availability of a host of different national foods throughout

countries of the North clearly give the lie to any suggestion that the choice available to global palates is less rather than more than it was two or three decades ago.

Evidence such as this, however, could be seen as superficial and not really engaging with the central argument of those who might happily acknowledge that there was as much movement from South to North – from periphery to centre in some terminologies – as in the other direction, but would again insist that what underlay the transfer in both cases was a system of commodity exchange which was essentially capitalist in structure and in ideology. However the actual movement of the flows was now operating, they would claim, what underpinned the system was the export from global centres of a way of looking at society and human relationships which ultimately exercised a monopoly on moral values and bulldozed to one side any competing lifestyles in its path. In this view technology transfer and the creation of the global consumer are not value-free but insidiously limit the choice of how one wishes to live. This is in some respects a difficult argument to refute, since it does seem to be self-evident that, with the exception of individuals or small alternative communities, once societies around the world have been exposed to the availability of products which promise to raise their quality of life, and understand what is required by the rules which have to be followed to achieve possession of those products – in the present state of the world at least this means a strong commitment to private ownership – then they will inevitably become to a greater or lesser extent free-market capitalists.

One response to such an account of the spread of capitalism might be that this need not be an entirely gloomy prospect, if the opportunities opened up by it can be interpreted as an enormous step forward in the liberation of peoples throughout the world whose present prospects are stunted and repressed. Lifestyles which currently restrict the scope for women to play a full and active role in their current social environments or deny children opportunities to develop their full potential and capacity for self-understanding are surely not to be defended simply in the interests of diversity. Marx himself was only too happy to see capitalism as a necessary step in the evolution to socialism. Perhaps a stronger line of argument, however, is to show by a closer look at the transfer of structures, knowledge and values that the ideology is not so universally powerful as it may seem, and that the process of transferring world-views is considerably more complex than has been allowed. For one thing, world-views, like cultures, are constantly evolving and cannot be pinned down to a definitive set of characteristics. Thus, although it may be analytically useful in economic theory to define a particular mode of extracting economic surplus as capitalist, it is entirely misleading to extend the definition to a capitalist view of the world, since there is simply no once-and-for-all view that corresponds to the economic concept. (It is partly this apparent lack of congruence between economic models and general world-views that has recently led to the phenomenon that in Britain capitalism, in the form of increasing privatization, can be promoted by a party claiming to be socialist and opposed by a party allegedly conservative.)

Furthermore, one can adduce a number of examples, some perhaps trivial and relatively unimportant, but also some quite weighty and compelling, to show that in fact there is much of substance which has made its way from the periphery and which is not only being absorbed into the cultures of the centre but also transforming them. The diversity of cuisines may well not be in this respect a good instance, since its influence on fundamental orientations to the world may not be great, but one can point to the increasing significance of alternative philosophies, many of exogenous origin, not only on individual lifestyles but also on the policies of political parties in governments of the North. Environmental and green issues of greater or lesser significance have made a considerable impact on the political imaginations of the electorates. In matters of health and the treatment of illness, too, it could be argued that the growing tendency in Western medicine to adopt a holistic attitude to patients owes much to observations on the part of the medical profession and to laypersons that alternative therapies and dietary regimes, many of them coming from non-Western medical systems, have much to commend them. That this should be so should not surprise us since, as the tag *ex oriente lux* reminds us, within the period of early modern European history scientific ideas from the East have had a profound significance on the development of modern sciences.

The debate, therefore, is not whether cultural flows can move in opposite directions and whether the specific direction of movement at any particular period is dependent on the historical configuration of political forces engaged in negotiating structures of wealth and power, but the degree to which the flows from periphery to centre significantly affect lifestyles, opportunities and collective social goals, and whether the present global situation is so much more qualitatively different from anything which has preceded it that appeal to historical precedent is invalid. Such questions can only really be answered with historical hindsight, and however strong our claims in a priori terms of structural inevitability, there is still, at least seen from the end of the twentieth century, a strong element of unpredictability, which in the short term must confound theorists of convergency and diversity alike. However, putting aside the long-term question of historical continuity and radical change, we need to make the best sense we can of the policies now being adopted world-wide by national governments which are explicitly designed to counter the movement towards transnational political central governance and monocultural unification.

The British government's move towards devolution offers an especially apt example occurring at the very time when Britain, in the eyes of some critical observers, is in danger of losing its political sovereignty and, with it, its sense of national identity through increasing amalgamation within the European Union. Through the creation of local assemblies in Wales and Scotland the government is pursuing a strategy of decentralization while at the same time appearing to surrender much of its central powers to a transnational authority. Of course, in terms of governance there is nothing inconsistent in this policy. The European Union itself encourages local devolution to regions in the interests of more precisely targeted economic development policies. Furthermore, in some countries of the Union where there are strong separatist movements – among the Catalans in Spain, for example – this trend to decentralization can be regarded as a means of extending substantial political autonomy without sacrificing national unity. If separatists can be persuaded that a significant number of their demands are being met within the new structures, then the hope is that they will be willing to accept the ultimate authority of national government. The trick is to balance the relinquishment of powers with retention of control and at the same time convince the regions of the sincerity of one's motives. The last is a particularly difficult feat when the history of the relations between centre and region has been one of distrust and betrayal leading to struggle, resistance and violent repression that still lives on in the memories of contemporary participants – a situation which we are only too familiar with in the world today in nations ranging from Canada and the USA to Yugoslavia, France (with its problems in Corsica), Nigeria, Congo, the Philippines (with its problems in the southern islands of the archipelago) and China.

The present difficulties in Indonesia arising from tensions between central government in Jakarta and the province of Aceh in north Sumatra graphically illustrate this problem. In the latter half of the nineteenth century the Acehnese fought heroically against the Dutch as they tried to resist colonial conquest. Ultimately they were defeated, but the memory of that struggle remained a powerful image in the collective Acehnese consciousness. When the opportunity to throw off the yoke of colonialism came in 1945 with the establishment of the Republic of Indonesia the Acehnese were happy to cast in their lot with the Republic. Once the Dutch had conceded independence to Indonesia, however, there arose the question of Aceh's place within the new Republic, and for a time in the 1950s an Acehnese separatist movement caused problems for the new government. Eventually, through a combination of political negotiation and military action, a compromise was reached whereby Aceh would be considered within the Republic as a 'region of special status', giving the Acehnese limited autonomy. In practice, however, this concession of autonomy was never really implemented and over the years the central government, using both military and civil institutions, became increasingly interventionist in Aceh, among other things exercising tight control over much of the export revenue which Aceh earned. Inevitably this led to a resurgence of separatist sentiment which in the 1980s was repressed with ever greater brutality by the regime of President Suharto. Against this background the new government of President Abdurrahman Wahid, elected in 1999, has a formidable struggle on its hands in now convincing the Acehnese that it is genuine in its desire to grant real autonomy to Aceh within the framework of the Indonesian nation: the legacy of the recent past exerts a powerful influence on the Acehnese imagination.

Paradoxically, the situation in Britain seems to be one of persuading regions to take on more responsibility for themselves. Having accepted the economic argument that devolution is good for economic development, the government's task now appears to be to convince the majority of the populations in the regions, beginning with Scotland and Wales, that perhaps the nationalists did have a point after all. The problem has arisen in this case because the tradition of parliamentary democracy with national elections every five years has eroded a sense of participation in government and created apathy at a local level. It is this apathy which the government is now seeking to overcome – with, it must be confessed, only limited success to date.

On the surface the apparent lack of enthusiasm of the electorate for a separate Welsh political identity in particular must come as a surprise, since the images of a Welsh cultural identity are so strong. These range from regular celebrations of Welsh traditions of singing associated both with individual performers and with community choirs and cultural festivals, to a commitment to the Welsh rugby team. By far the most powerful of these institutions of Welshness, however, is the Welsh language itself, and in this respect over the last half century the establishment of Welsh-medium schools and the creation of a Welsh-language television station are testimony to the extraordinary revival of the language. Why is it, however, that these successful projections of Welshness have not been matched by a corresponding enthusiasm for a Welsh assembly? To pose the question in this way, however, immediately suggests an answer and at the same time raises more general philosophical questions about the obligations and limits of a government's commitment to multiculturalism.

What appears to be a lack of interest, at least as measured in polling statistics, can be explained by the fact that although there is a large constituency of people who welcome the initiatives to create or reinforce a sense of Welsh identity and who applaud the efforts made through language policies in schools and throughout the civil service to promote Welsh, there is an equally large constituency which is indifferent if not hostile to these policies which they regard as not touching upon their own personal sense of identity. A geographical division between North and South, or, from a border perspective, between East and West, corresponding with historical patterns of settlement has a critical influence on how one responds to the notion of Welshness (Bowie 1993). The cities of the south, with their strong traditions of attracting migrant labour from not only England but also other countries of Europe, while happily prepared to support to the hilt the Welsh rugby team, strongly resist any move to compulsory Welsh-language initiatives.

As long as these divisions can be geographically contained, the differences present no problem to the government. Welsh-medium schools for Welsh-language speakers in the North and English-medium schools in the South. However, the division is not quite so neat, and anyway what does one do with the preference that individuals might express for wanting their children educated in English-medium schools when they reside in a Welsh-speaking area? The issue of choice at this point becomes crucial. With television channels the individual has a range of options and can decide whether to watch television in Welsh or English. If, however, there are no local English-medium schools in a Welsh-speaking area, where does the government's responsibility lie in providing such schools? This is a difficult dilemma and not one solved by the easy answer that anyone living in a Welsh-speaking area must abide by local conditions – one of which is the language medium of the schools – or must get out. Such a response begins to smack of social apartheid and, besides creating rifts along cultural and possibly class lines, also risks ostracizing or at least alienating those members of the community who may not want to follow all the community's prescriptions. This issue of separation and division has a significance well beyond the immediate Welsh case – still in Britain, for example, these same issues are discussed very perceptively in relation to the revival of Gaelic in Scotland by Macdonald (1997) – and applies to all those who may want to deviate from strict religious observance in those ethnic communities where such observance is a criterion for membership, as discussed at some length by Kymlicka (1995).

There are no easy formulaic prescriptions which can be universally applied, and again and again we see that it is almost always specific contingent circumstances which will determine where justice and equity reside; nevertheless, we can identify one or two areas where multicultural policies need to be thought through in terms of general principles. A first question one might ask is whether a government should intervene in order to endorse or encourage multiculturalism, either because it regards cultural diversity and difference as a good *per se*, or because it wishes to protect the interests of minorities which are in danger of being subordinated to the dominant populations at national or regional levels. If intervention is appropriate, what form should it take: legislation, social engineering, affirmative action, the offer of economic incentives, or simply the provision of minimal facilities which increase the range of options available to individuals to retain or establish a specific ethnic identity within the structure of the state? These two questions and the set of issues they subsume will always constitute the core of considerations which policy-makers should consider, but for observers of the process there is another crucial consideration which policy-makers sometimes disguise in their public support for multiculturalism, that is, what are the specific interests of governments which policies are designed to achieve and are these interests coincidental with the interests of the minorities themselves? The relevance of this question can be illustrated by example.

As we have already noted, the policy of the Chinese state towards minorities from imperial times up to the present has always been to encourage the rapid assimilation into Han Chinese culture, the dominant culture of the nation whose members are alleged to share common descent from the Han people.[4] This tendency was accelerated after the communist revolution since in the eyes of the communists the cultural traditions of minorities were additionally despised for harking back either to pre-capitalist and feudal regimes or linked to primitive stages of cultural development. Consequently, it was the state's task to educate people out of their narrow parochial vision of their own cultures to a proud identification with, and commitment to, Chinese Communism – of the Han variety. With the ending of the Cultural Revolution, however, there has been a noticeable shift in government policy and now ethnic minorities are being encouraged to demonstrate and celebrate their individuality through the promotion of their unique lifestyles, visible in their costumes and in their local customs and traditions. Furthermore, the state's recognition that they are not Han involves an ipso facto recognition that they need special privileges, in the educational field and in relation to political representation, to enable them to enjoy the same access to new development opportunities as the Han. The upshot of this policy is often confusion and uncertainty at a local level. On the one hand government officials are proud to be seen encouraging the festivals and cultural performances of minority peoples, but on the other they feel uneasy at the interest which outsiders take in these minorities, fearful that the foreign observer might later represent China as consisting of ignorant and primitive peoples. At the national level the government uses political opportunities to demonstrate for the benefit of international audiences an openness to multicultural variety within the nation, but at the same time domestically it seems to hold these minorities in contempt, using opportunities to exploit their cultures by representing them in exhibitions and films in a way designed to titillate the Han population – by suggesting, for example, that the women are sexually freely available (Gladney 1999). All the while the government also watches uneasily lest local pride in difference should threaten national unity.[5]

How, then, in this instance are we to judge the Chinese government's intentions? Is the apparent endorsement of ethnic minorities a strong statement in favour of multiculturalism, and does it represent a belief in the value of diversity and the right of individuals within the nation to express their identity through ethnic differentiation? Or do we do better to see the policy as essentially a form of tokenism designed for the sake of good international relations and in fact representing nothing more than a cynical manipulation of ethnic identities? Or, even more sinisterly, can we perceive here an attempt to undermine or pre-empt claims to sovereignty and independence on the part of those regions of China which regard themselves as colonies rather than integral parts of the nation? By allowing them to flaunt their minority cultural status and channel their energies into the representation and demonstration of that identity, is the government distracting attention away from demands for political autonomy or independence?

However one judges this specific Chinese example, it is undoubtedly the case that in many countries of the world the recent state sponsorship of minority cultures in terms of their historical legacies, their cultural artefacts or their contemporary institutions is designed to mollify the critical voices which might otherwise be making more substantial demands of government. In Canada, museums now focus on alternative perspectives of the country's historical tradition, from the viewpoint of the native North American peoples; in Indonesia in the Taman Mini, a huge theme park cum heritage site in Jakarta, cultural traditions from all over the archipelago are on exhibition and celebrated in display and performance; in Thailand, model villages of Highland minorities make available for tourists traditional handicrafts manufactured by people still wearing colourful 'traditional' costume (Yamashita _et al._ 1997); and in the Highlands of Scotland, crofters are taught the ancient skill of tweed-making so that they can demonstrate a highland tradition for a television programme.

In one way or another all these enterprises – and there has been an explosive growth of such theme parks and heritage sites throughout the world in the 1980s and 1990s – point to the actions of governments trying to colonize or at least to contain opposition almost by stealth, by promoting a multicultural view of the nation at the same time as courting the allegiance of the minority group which might otherwise see itself as dispossessed – culturally, economically, socially – by the government. Yet to make that judgement is to be guilty of the same charge as that levelled against those who argue that colonialism makes for uniformity and is blind to the creative ability of groups and individuals to transform institutions and give them new meaning. With reference to the Highlands of Scotland mentioned above, for example, Macdonald (1997: 108–11) has shown very effectively how the Highland women were very much aware of the absurdity of the role they were being asked to play but were able to turn it to their own advantage, establishing in the process a strong and well-managed women's group. Similarly, the 'gentle highlanders' in Thailand know full well how to play the game to their own advantage without becoming pawns in the strategy of central government.

The whole weight of evidence seems to point, then, to a constantly evolving and changing set of cultural forms which defy any attempt to manipulate them directly through government intervention or indirectly through the invisible hand of global capitalist enterprise. At every turn, just as forms appear to be fixed, they reveal on closer examination to be still metamorphosing. Even in the case of those religious traditions which might appear to be immutable and indeed which lay such stress on immutability – in the attention to a historically fixed scriptural authority, for example – change and alteration can be readily perceived. Any other interpretation of the process of cultural transformation, one which, for example, deplores the convergence of cultures to a single USA-dominated model, labours under two principal misconceptions: that a culture can be represented as some reified essence with specific characteristics and qualities which make it unique and incapable of change except at the expense of its own disappearance; and that a historically shallow synchronic description of events offers sufficient evidence to allow us to evaluate the shape and direction of change. As a correction to such misconceptions we need to remind ourselves that the Heraclitean observation that all is flux applies as much to cultural form as to any other human endeavour, and that consequently, for a better perspective on contemporary cultural phenomena, we would be well advised to locate them within a comparative historical framework.

Notes

1 For a fascinating description of how this is now happening in Chinese cities see Bin Zhao (1997).
2 John Gray (1999) is particularly hard on this argument, which is associated with Francis Fukuyama; see also David Apter (1999) for similar points.
3 For some passionate recent arguments about the way in which culture and the economy are imbricated and whether the current intellectual focus on culture and the politics of recognition is displacing attention away from where it should be focused, that is, on the political economy, see the discussion between Fraser and Young in the *New Left Review*, well summarized and commented on by Phillips (1997).
4 See Gladney (1991: 293–337) for a critical account of this process and the myth of Han homogeneity.
5 Although not an ethnic minority, the treatment meted out to the Falun Gong sect illustrates the point here. The Chinese government is pleased to be seen as tolerating the practice of religion and relaxing the persecution which was so prominent a characteristic of the Cultural Revolution, yet when the religion poses a challenge then it must be severely dealt with.

Multiculturalism in Historical Perspective

The close attention now paid to multiculturalism – or rather, the labelling as multiculturalism of a range of issues relating to ethnicity, religious practice and cultural expression which governments must directly respond to in the formulation of policies – at first sight may appear to be a development of the late twentieth century, which has arisen both as a consequence of the rapid creation of new nations and the accelerated pace of geographical mobility made possible through advances in transport technology. On closer examination, however, this appearance may be deceptive since though the label and the slant of the discussion may be new, the issues themselves are historically familiar. The mobility of populations is as old as the history of humanity itself, and states and nations in the past have always had to confront the problems arising from the diversity of groups within one polity. While making due allowance, therefore, for the difference in scale to which twentieth-century developments have given rise, it is essential to introduce a dimension of historical comparison to contemporary discussions.

Military conquest and subsequent territorial expansion are the ways most familiar to us through which ethnic groups have spread their cultural influence. We have seen above how Chinese civilization imposed itself on the territories which became at one time or another part of the Chinese empire. Vietnam, for example, for the period corresponding to the first Christian millennium was heavily influenced by Chinese models which dominated institutions of government and created a bureaucratic elite which not only in its outlook and thinking but even in its language orientation was thoroughly Chinese, so much so that even after a thousand years of independence from China that influence is still strong.

Military conquest by an ethnic group does not, however, necessarily mean that the cultural outlook of the conqueror inevitably imposes itself on the other, as again the Chinese example shows. The Chinese imperial dynasties which originated outside the Han heartland, the Mongol Yuan (1276–1368) and in particular the Manchu Qing (1644–1912), very quickly exchanged their own life-styles in preference for the Chinese models which they recognized had advantages over their own. Similarly, even though the Romans had made Greece part of their colonial empire, rather than suppress Greek culture and civilization they in fact adopted it as a model for their own practice. However, even in looking at these cases where the evidence of cultural borrowing and adoption seems clear, we must again be careful not to fall into the trap of reifying culture and regarding it as some sort of fixed and finite commodity which can be consumed or taken up in the way in which the descriptions above suggest. Culture is above everything a congeries of ways of thinking and acting which, however much they may appear to be the commonly shared experience of a collectivity of people and attempts are made to define them as such, are constantly being modified and transformed. It is therefore misleading to apply national labels to culture as though they represented some unchanging essence: what passes for British (or French or Spanish or Chinese or Hindu) culture today, however one tries to identify its characteristics, very rarely resembles what passed under the same label a century before. We can perceive something of the complex way in which the changes occur if we take another example of the diffusion of cultural influence after conquest.

After the Norman invasion of 1066 there was a considerable influx of French ideas and cultural habits into Britain, brought not only by the Norman nobility but also by the artisans, merchants, clerics and soldiers who came in their wake (Stenton 1951). This tide of French – or rather Norman – culture exerted a powerful influence on the development of English civilization at all levels of society as a consequence of the introduction of new legal and political institutions and the development of important economic links, not to mention changes wrought in the ecclesiastical establishment. The changes did not, however, occur in one fell swoop, and the process through which Norman institutions permeated English life and thought was a matter of decades and centuries rather than months and years. Furthermore, throughout this period Norman culture did not remain impervious to change but was itself influenced by conditions which it encountered in England. Thus, rather than one culture or way of life superseding or displacing another, we find instead a slow growing together of ideas, knowledge, private habits and public ways of behaving, leading to a unique constellation of cultural characteristics manifested in everything from patterns of domestic consumption and styles of architecture, to systems of government, tenurial arrangements for property, legal institutions, literary genres and dramatic performances.

Following the typology which the American anthropologist, Robert Redfield (1954), developed to explain the coexistence of cultural difference within one nation, one might be tempted to account for what was happening in such a process as the Norman Conquest as the product of a division created between a Great Tradition, found in court and urban centres where there was a conscious elaboration of social norms and formal rituals, and a Little Tradition, found in villages and in rural areas in general, where there are simpler codes of behaviour. The two traditions are taken to be largely separate, although they do come into contact and there is even a mutual borrowing between them in terms of styles of dress, cultural performance and even religious practice. In such a view the towns of Norman England would be repositories of French influence drawing their inspiration from the court of the king, while the villages would still have been pursuing their Anglo-Saxon lifestyles unaffected by changes in administrative and cultural centres. Although such a view allows us to distinguish different lifestyles and look for characteristics of social class and areas of residence, we now tend to regard this dichotomy between great and little traditions with some misgivings since it obscures the way in which cultural forms are constantly evolving. Thus it is misleading to regard town and village as somehow mutually exclusive, each pursuing its own cultural path in a form of cultural dualism. Although superficially the observation that one has to deal with two distinctive language communities, that of the French-speaking court and its imitators and that of the Anglo-Saxon speaking villagers, the appeal to language as an indicator of heterogeneity, taken over the longer period, is deceptive too, since in fact what we find is a slow coming together of French and Anglo-Saxon into what becomes by the early modern period a recognizable modern

English. The development of the language into a unique form of verbal expression in this way, rather than representing a division and separation of cultures, provides an illustration of the manner in which disparate cultural influences can play upon each other to generate new possibilities.

This constant evolution of changing forms as a result of what used to be called 'culture contact' can and frequently does occur historically in cases where it is not military conquest which has been the engine of transformation, but trade and commercial opportunity. One of the most spectacular examples of this is to be found in the so-called Indianization of the countries of Southeast Asia (Coedes 1948). Exactly how this process occurred is still, despite the careful scholarship devoted to the issue, largely a mystery, and the reference to Indianization is perhaps as misleading as references to the Normanization of England, but we can see very clearly how in the space of a thousand years or more, again around the period of the first Christian millennium, religious beliefs and cosmologies, together with their accompanying scriptural texts and architectural and artistic monuments, spread throughout the region. Thus kingdoms and petty states were set up modelled on, though not necessarily slavishly imitating, Hindu structures and institutions and employing principles of economic and political organization which sought their legitimacy in Hindu precedent. This whole process, which had a geographical distribution from Burma to Bali, has left a profound impression on Southeast Asian societies today as even the most cursory observations of artefacts and lifestyles within the region reveal. But as far as we know, this process did not take place as a consequence of military conquest or as the result of any systematically planned strategy of the dissemination of influence. Furthermore, despite the thoroughgoing adoption of forms which superficially resemble their Hindu models, what we find on close study is not only that the slow fusion of cultural forms of exogenous and endogenous origins has led to new interpretations of earlier narratives, and the reworking of legacies of mythical and artistic traditions, which is where perhaps we might have expected it, but also that even in the interstices of everyday life, in the institutions of kinship and marriage for example, new forms have arisen, vestigially partaking of the principles and practices of what were once separate cultural philosophies.

These examples of the transformation of cultures, however, may not altogether convince those who doubt the commensurability of the experience of the twentieth century with the *longue durée* of previous historical periods, where change was not only relatively much slower but also qualitatively different. In response to such objections we need, then, to turn to the modern period to note how the same operations of cultural transformation still obtain even in circumstances where governments now engage in considerably more systematic forms of social engineering than in the pre-modern period.

At the end of the nineteenth century, despite the appearance of a unified British culture and a strong sense of British identity fuelled by the successful pursuit of a colonial empire overseas and the consolidation of the industrial revolution at home – not to mention a strong commitment to Protestantism which Linda Colley (1992: 367–9) mentions as perhaps the most important single factor in unifying the nation – there were clearly differences in the ways in which the population of the country experienced that Britishness and felt themselves part of the nation. Those differences in large part related to positions within the class structure or to the region of the country in which people resided. However, throughout that century a noticeable process of homogenization had been brought about by the spread of communications which had done much to disseminate the sharing of a common culture. Newspapers were commonly available, education and literacy had given people access to a knowledge of the national and international contexts of the times in which they lived, and the standardization of the language and universal recognition of the literary giants of the culture of the past and present – from Shakespeare, Pope and Johnson to Dickens and Scott, Wordsworth and Tennyson – not to mention the heritage of the Bible and the textual tradition of English Christian writing, had brought about some cultural unification to complement the uniformity of political and economic institutions. Furthermore, with respect to religious minorities, the exclusion of Catholics and Jews from participation in political life had become, thanks to the emancipation Acts, a thing of the past, and Jews and Catholics were happy to show their gratitude for this new tolerance by overt demonstrations of their Englishness. However, at the same time immigrant communities were still arriving and settling in the country in significant numbers (Anderson 1990: 6–9; Thompson 1990: 49–55). In their distinctive ways of life and in the residential areas in which they settled they represented, in so far as they became visible to the population at large, not so much an alien presence as a certain degree of otherness. Jews from central and eastern Europe, bringing with them a very different lifestyle from the Spanish Sephardic community already largely assimilated, Italian migrants, both political exiles from an earlier period and economic migrants practising distinctive trades, Irish workers, Chinese and Indian sailors (McFarland 1991) who had settled in port towns and a handful of Eastern students and businessmen some of whom were entering British political life, all were con-tributing in one way or another to the changing contours of the landscape of British society.

Although it would be wrong to deny that there were incidents of racist violence arising from what was perceived at a local level to be unfair economic competition (Howell and Baber 1990: 319), the spirit of the first few decades of the twentieth century was one of relative tolerance.[1] There was an implicit mutual understanding on the part of the new migrant populations and the host com-munities that within two or three generations the migrants whose languages and habits now appeared so alien would have acquired an appropriate mastery of English ways, and would no longer appear out of place, however much of their original culture they retained within the privacy of their homes and their places of worship. Their difference, consequently, would not be publicly visible and hence they would become thoroughly integrated within British society as generations of immigrants had before them; and like those earlier generations they too, in their individual ways, would enrich the cultural life of the nation in a manner ranging from additions to the cuisine of the country to different kinds of professional specialization. This of course is, by and large, what indeed happened with Irish and Italian and, to a lesser extent, Jewish migrants. Where physical appearance was noticeably different – in relation to the skin colour of Asians and Africans – the process of integration was perhaps not quite so seamless, but before the second half of the century, the number of Asian and African immigrants was relatively small and at least within the communities in which they resided individuals were able to estab-lish an identity for themselves on the basis of their own singular personalities rather than as representatives of ethnic groups or members of a specific religious persuasion.

This situation changed dramatically in the 1950s – this period is well covered in Hiro (1991) – when an increasing number of Com-monwealth migrants came to take up the slack in the labour force in the British economy and began to set up small but highly visible communities in London and in major industrial towns in the North of England. Although the statistics and sociology of this Common-wealth migration have frequently been presented and discussed and various forms of documentary have recorded the experience of the new immigrants, to my mind there has been little satisfactory explanation of the shifting attitudes of the host population over this period beyond occasional reference to growing hostility reflected in incidents such as the Notting Hill race riots in 1958. Two closely related and highly significant factors have not been given the atten-tion they deserve and warrant further research: first, the cultural lag in the representation of other cultures, namely *fin de siècle* intel-lectual opinions only trickling down to the popular imagination in the second half of the century; and second, a corresponding shift away from an unspoken pressure on immigrant populations to become Anglicized to one which required immigrants to keep to themselves and abide by the rules rather than attempt the imposs-ible of becoming Englishmen.

The first of these is relatively easy to document. The films and popular novels and magazines of the time, with their references to Tarzan, Jungle Jim and King Solomon's mines, as well as films such as *Beau Geste* and *Kim* portraying eastern bazaars and Chinese opium dens, all created a suspicion of, and a sedimented contempt for, the non-European. This imagining of the non-European other as alien and alternately threatening or ridiculous built on images already constructed from stereotypical traits attributed to non-British Europeans. To these were added further dimensions of difference in terms of physical appearance and pagan beliefs and superstitions, all of which derived from descriptions of a previous generation of writers. Nor was that imagining of the Oriental and African other as lacking in the culture and civilization of the Chris-tian West confined to popular fiction; a very similar but more sophisticated and elaborate fictional crafting was being perpetrated in works which portrayed the fag-end of colonialism – novels by Graham Greene, Evelyn Waugh and Joyce Cary, for example. Added to this, although the process of decolonialization was a rela-tively benign affair in the British colonies, the negative represen-tation of nationalist politicians and the quick resort to inflammatory epithets – terrorists, saboteurs, communists – and the disturbing references to acts of barbarism and violence had the cumulative effect of distancing the European from the non-European and

confirming those Victorian images of benighted savagery in desperate need of Western enlightenment.[2]

Even when the non-European other was represented sympathetically, it was either in the guise of the trusty servant or the
Anglophile aristocrat, and in both cases the image for public consumption encouraged an amused contempt, a tolerance of the ludicrous and the pretentious, of the kind fostered in much of the
earlier literature of Kipling, Haggard and, dare one say it, Conrad.
Such representations, often further confirmed by the anecdotal
references of pensioned colonial officials now at large in the Britain
of the 1950s, fed into a growing conviction that non-white others
were all right in their place, but they should not try to reach beyond
themselves, either through social mobility or through intermarriage. It was this new conceptualization which, among other factors
such as the changing economic conditions of the time, led to a sense
of separateness and the desire to maintain social and cultural difference, while at the same time closely monitoring the strict adherence
of the other to social conventions and national laws. Consequently,
when Roy Jenkins, the then Home Secretary, in 1966 made his now
well-known case for a policy of integration rather than assimilation
(Grillo 1998: 177), his argument matched both growing popular
sentiment and liberal intellectual views both of which, while
perhaps springing from different assessments of the status of the
other, were dangerously predicated on a sense of quintessential
difference.

The opinions developed in this critical period in race relations in
Britain still strongly colour attitudes in the country to multiculturalism. Though the term may be recent, and though there have
been immense demographic changes in the socio-economic composition of British society, it can plausibly be argued that the
debates about freedom of religious expression, multilingual education and the nature of entrenched racism in British social and
political institutions all derive from tortuous attempts to reconcile
a principle of difference with one of equality. This, of course, is a
problem which concerns not only ethnic groups but also social
classes and distinctive communities of religious believers as well as
gays and lesbians. At one level the demand for equality of treatment in the public sphere is directed against institutional racism
and seems to represent a plea for colour-blindness. At the same
time a slightly more radical, and certainly a more realistic argument
suggests that such a demand for equality can only be satisfactorily

met by fulfilling certain preconditions which will allow access to all the social and educational facilities which the society has to offer, and that the realization of this particular condition requires intervention and affirmative action on the part of government. Consequently, debates should not be about whether one should engage in forms of positive discrimination but how, and in particular whether there can be a confluence of interests at the level of class and social exclusion which transcends issues of cultural, religious and colour difference. A further twist to the debates, however, denies the premises of both liberal and the radical arguments, both of which imply an ultimate convergence towards some universal model to which all in good time will subscribe. This final position argues strongly that there should be room within the state for cultural difference which might extend beyond the private domestic realm into areas of public worship, education and even family law. Thus the state should not only allow people freedom to profess whatever religion they choose, but also facilitate the expression of religious faith by, for example, expanding the scope of state-supported religious education, granting building permissions for places of worship, and in due course making special provision for, say, polygamous marriage within religious communities where this is sanctioned. The opponents of this latter position argue vehemently against these demands, alleging their illiberalism and their grounding in a denial of civil rights, in effect taking a stand on the limits of the right of communities to be different.

At the same time as these debates reverberate in government chambers and find their way into policy documents and committee reports as well as into discussion programmes and polemics in the media, changes in the demographic profile of the country are also gradually modifying perceptions of possibilities within cultural and inter-ethnic relations – see Alibhai-Brown (1999), though she argues persuasively that the change in attitudes is too slow. Mixed marriages, once so frowned upon, though still not common, frequently occur; it is no longer a novelty to encounter non-white people in high positions of public office and being counted among the good and the great of the land. A new generation of novelists includes among its foremost names black and Asian writers, as well as white authors whose accounts of other cultures are not simply more nuanced than previous examples, but written with a different dimension of understanding and exposition of far greater insight than anything which has gone before. In the entertainment world,

bhangra, rap and reggae are now not simply alternative but constitute mainstream music; films and television programmes have parts
for non-white actors and are produced by a growing body of black
and Asian British professionals, and the subject matter of the
dramas and the satire also draws on the lives of the non-white populations.

There is, then, good reason to argue that collectively British
society is undergoing a major change in its attitude to cultural diversity, and that the constantly recurring debates about the appropri-
ateness or otherwise of state intervention and the design of policies
of multiculturalism, although not immediately resolving the conflicting views expressed within British society, indicate the health of
democratic traditions of open discussion. However, it would be
wrong to over-exaggerate the speed and depth of the changes which
are taking place. Enquiries such as the Macdonald report into the
stabbing of an Asian-British schoolboy in Manchester and the
Macpherson report into the killing of the black teenager, Stephen
Lawrence, make sombre reading for anyone inclined to have an
optimistic view of the current situation. It is also true that there is
still overt racism on the football terraces (*The Guardian*, 7 January
2000; see also Holland 1995). Furthermore, those extensive and
damaging representations of other cultures produced in the 1950s
continue to linger on in the popular imagination and are still being
transmitted down the generations, sometimes finding corroborative
reinforcement in the contemporary screen descendants of the
tradition – Indiana Jones and James Bond for the representation
of foreign villains and Anna and the King of Siam for the well-
intentioned but ludicrous foreign potentate. Moreover, although
debates on multiculturalism are now given considerable airing in
the media, the quality of the presentation of the issues leaves much
to be desired: the temptation to sensationalize and caricature is
rarely resisted, and the structure of discussion programmes, with
their reliance on adversarial sound-bites, militates against any real
exposition of difficult problems. There is still far too little general
understanding of other cultural traditions within British society,
and television and radio in particular do not make the most of their
opportunities.[3] Nevertheless, even from a position of scepticism,
one can see that at least a context and an expectation of debate on
those crucial issues of identity as they relate to culture, education
and religious practice have been created.

The historical background to similar debates and discussion in the USA has been substantially different and, as we might have anticipated, the issues which have come to the forefront of public consciousness also differ. If the watershed in shifting attitudes to the assimilation of migrant communities occurred in Britain as a consequence of the influx of New Commonwealth immigrants in the 1950s which brought about a rethinking of the nature of social expectations and cultural conventions and an interrogation of what precisely constituted Britishness, one can argue that the major watershed in Americans' perceptions of themselves was occurring at more or less the same time, the late 1950s, not so much as a consequence of new immigration but as a direct result of the civil rights movement.

At the risk of over-simplification, one can argue that prior to the impact of the civil rights movement, questions of American identity and culture had been framed in terms of what were sometimes competing and sometimes complementary accounts of the nation deriving from two sources. The first and most influential was the Anglo-American tradition associated with the founding fathers of the Republic, which combined Enlightenment traditions of the eighteenth century with both a Protestant ethic of Puritan communities and the more luxurious lifestyles of a wealthy plantocracy. Christian morality, Western scientific thought, French manners and an English style of expression in not only language but also institutions characterized this culture, most succinctly captured in the autobiographies of men such as Benjamin Franklin. Set against this and contributing a second but not so pronounced account of Americanness was the culture of the immigrants from Ireland, Scandinavia, Germany, central Europe and the Mediterranean countries, especially Italy, and also from the Far East. Each of these immigrant communities brought with it its own distinctive religious traditions, economic orientations and patterns of family relationships and communal sense of identity. Being so distinctive and different from one another they shared little in common, and certainly nothing which they could in any united fashion set up in opposition to the dominant Anglo-Protestant tradition which they found already well established by the end of the nineteenth century. There was, one might claim, a common pioneering spirit of enterprise and a desperate desire to succeed which drove all the new migrants and a feeling of gratitude and relief that they were able to do so in circumstances, especially away from the east coast, where they could both declare themselves proudly American and yet pursue, albeit in a modified and constantly adaptive manner, the cultural mores which they carried with them from their countries of origin.

By the second decade of the twentieth century the second and third generation of the pioneer immigrants had become sufficiently Americanized to the point where, although the commitment to an American identity remained fiercely strong, the overwhelming sense of gratitude which had been the dominant sentiment felt by their parents had now been replaced by a sense of pride and confidence. Increasingly they had come to recognize that their communities had not just received the benefits of, but made substantial contributions to, American prosperity and to what was being commonly referred to as American way of life, favourably distinguishable from anything left behind in Europe. In that spirit of confidence engendered by their sense of accomplishment, various challenges were mounted against the supremacy of the Anglo-Protestant. Irish Catholics, for example, began to create a political constituency of their own in the cities of the east; German-Jewish migrants (Hornung 1998: 216–24) lobbied for the recognition of Jewish traditions.[4]

Concurrently the black population of the country, represented by men like Bourne and Du Bois, also began to assert a sense of identity and cultural and historical distinctiveness which had gone unrecognized in the debates about Americanness. Given the nascent state of American culture at the time, there was every opportunity for these demands from different communities to register their presence in the nation at large, particularly with respect to forms of expression which posed no challenge to the dominant political and religious creeds. Thus music and art were very quickly welcomed as contributing to a sense of distinctive American vitality, as the incorporation of jazz and blues and the whole movement known as the Harlem renaissance – though jazz was not a major element of the latter – illustrates (Kahn 1995: 109–16; Lively 1998: 203–46). It was during this period that we see the beginnings of what later came to be called a 'hyphenated identity'. Thus people began to regard themselves as Italian-American, Polish-American, Chinese-American and so on. This dual identity did not, however, impair or threaten a strong commitment to the democratic principles of the country or to its legal or educational institutions.

In the 1950s, however, those institutions were found wanting in the way in which they failed to provide adequately for the black population of the country, who protested loudly and vigorously but peacefully that Constitutional guarantees for the democratic rights of individuals were being ignored in their case and that this situation should immediately be rectified. As we know, not only was the civil rights movement, led by men of the stature of Martin Luther King, ultimately successful in seeing civil rights extended to the black population of the country, but the spectacular and dramatic way in which its campaigns were conducted led to a nationwide reappraisal of the nature of American identity and the position of minorities within the population. Moreover, in addition to encouraging a full-scale re-evaluation of the accepted traditions of American history with respect to the black slave population and a universal recognition of the deplorability of much of that history, inevitably this national soul-searching prompted a review of the manner in which the American Indians, now referred to as native Americans, had become the victims of a sometimes savage process of violent suppression, as came to be revealed through what became canonical accounts such as *Bury My Heart at Wounded Knee* (Brown 1971) and later in films such as *Little Big Man* and later again *Dancing with Wolves*. In turn, this new focus on the historical experience of minority populations prompted attention to those communities which had until then more or less escaped the notice of the purveyors of the American tradition, the textbook writers, the journalists, the film-makers and the intellectual classes in general, namely groups such as the Japanese-Americans and Chinese-Americans (Daniels 1993) who now became the subjects of research and gained recognition of the history of their community in substantial novels such as Amy Tan's *The Joy Luck* and David Guterson's *Snow Falling on Cedars* in the same way as, three generations before, the other pioneers had found a voice in the novels of Willa Cather.

This new national awareness of the experience of non-white communities and their special position within American society has subsequently led to new policy initiatives and to a determination to reconfigure the historical record, so that it takes due note of the experiences of those immigrant communities which had previously been erased or simply omitted from the official histories. Within the 1980s and 1990s two significant developments have emerged from this collective acknowledgement that the past and the future would have to be attended to by action in the present. The first of these has been to build upon the new historical interest by encouraging the notion of a cultural heritage, of a legacy from the past, which encompasses not only the rediscovery of the traditions and experience of minorities, but also the re-creation of the way of life of communities throughout the country in heritage sites, theme parks and museums. The second, a much more controversial development and more directly political, has been the introduction into the educational and employment sectors of policies of affirmative action to redress the inherent disadvantages from which minorities suffer as a consequence of their structural position within the economy. This latter policy is bound up with a far more wide-ranging attempt to raise awareness about issues of disempowerment in general by advocating ways of socially interrelating with others in speech and action which run counter to what has been common everyday practice. This new focus has become known as 'politically correct behaviour' and has drawn much adverse criticism in the past few years.

Heritage sites and theme parks are not confined to the USA but they have been especially developed there – indeed, long before the new political consciousness of multiculturalism became an issue, Disneyworld had attempted within its venues re-creations of early American communities, but in this case suitably packaged to present a romantic and comfortable gloss on the past. At another level of seriousness altogether, Franz Boas and his anthropology students at the turn of the last century had recognized that the way of life of native Americans was fast disappearing and, in relation to what became know as salvage anthropology, had made every effort to record in detail the way of life of the many different ethnic groups which then existed. Their efforts, summed up in detailed reports to the Smithsonian Institution in Washington and the collections deposited there, allow us to imagine and understand the cultures of the past in vivid detail. The new initiatives build upon these researches but try to enhance the quality of sympathetic understanding first of all by not minimizing the hardship and suffering of earlier communities, but also by encouraging a more direct tactile and sensory impression of the former way of life. Visitors are directly encouraged to follow the detailed history of events of the times through a variety of new audio-visual techniques which create highly realistic simulations and allow personal interaction with the exhibitions and displays. Through this combination of direct experience and the following of narrative cues, then, visitors are led to respect and understand the past. Controversy, however, frequently arises in relation to how that past is interpreted and represented. Laura Peers (1999) has shown, for example, how new attempts to portray frontier life no longer in terms of white pioneers in confrontation with native Americans but working together with them, often conflict with the desires of descendants of the latter employed on these sites to chronicle the decimation and destruction of their communities as a result of contact: another version of the clash between 'soft' and critical multiculturalism, with proponents of the latter insisting on the need to address contemporary injustices which originate from actions carried out in those times. (One might note in passing that similar issues and similar initiatives are evident in Canada and Australia with respect to heritage, injustice and, in particular, in the case of those two countries, land rights.)

It is precisely this issue of continuing injustice which has provided the spur for policies of affirmative action. It would take too long to provide the socio-economic evidence which explains the justification for these frequently misunderstood policies, but the general principle informing them is that various sections of the population in society are unable to take advantage of the opportunities for self-fulfilment which potentially the American democracy offers to all its citizens. They are hampered by cultural and poverty 'traps' which restrict their horizons and indirectly force them into a way of life in which they are condemned to perpetual structural subordination within the society.[5] To free them from these traps it is necessary to make special provision in education and employment to enable them to overcome the obstacles they face, and the obvious ways in which that can be done are by establishing ethnic quotas in university entrance and by monitoring employment especially in the public sector to ensure that ethnic minorities are not systematically suffering discrimination.

Opponents of such policies, especially in California where they have now been implemented for some time, angrily argue that the result of what has been done is to exchange one discrimination for another, and that now the children of the ethnic majorities are the ones who are suffering from limited access to prestigious schools of higher education or who are being turned down for jobs despite their qualifications. Affirmative action, in their opinion, whatever its justification in the past, needs now to be abandoned in the interests of justice to all. Two corollary points are often made in this context. First, the preference for weaker candidates – for higher education or for employment – in the interests of meeting quotas will ultimately lead to a drastic decline in educational standards and in the quality of public service, and this can be in no one's interests. Second, representatives from ethnic minorities themselves resent the implication that they require special consideration, since this inevitably means that they are recognized not for their individual talents and abilities, but as having reached their positions through a system of special privileging.[6] This may be a strong argument when it can be buttressed by systematic evidence, but too often the cases which come to attention are of a sensational and extreme kind and do not bear upon the major long-term issues of disempowerment and exclusion for which more systematic and longitudinal studies are required. The likelihood is very strong that when the evidence is sifted, the intricacies of the situation, and the difficulty of separating issues of history, class and different kinds of cultural experience will require neither a total rejection of affirmative action, nor a continuation of it in its present form, but a far more nuanced set of policies which understand the complexity and the variation within societies.

In comparing the issues which arise in discussions of multiculturalism in the USA and in Britain, one is struck as much by the differences as the similarities. In Britain, the arguments are largely about religious freedoms and, by extension, about the issue of special religious schools. Only to a secondary degree does the issue of social exclusion take on board, in the public perception at least, the ethnic or multicultural dimension of these issues, the principal concern in the USA. This is not for lack of trying on the part of bodies such as the Commission for Racial Equality, which is constantly bringing to court highly publicized cases of racist behaviour and discrimination. Nor, again in Britain, has there been any lack of campaigning in educational circles for dual language policies in areas with substantial ethnic minority communities. And in Census forms and official questionnaires data are now collected on the ethnic origin of respondents. There are, however, no attempts to introduce quota systems, and government policy, although not impervious to the seriousness of these issues and to charges of institutionalized racism, seems more alarmed by the alleged failure of the communities to integrate into the fabric of the nation and commit themselves to democratic objectives.[7] At a popular level, however, notwithstanding the ugly and still frequent displays of racism against the non-white population, one does find an extra-ordinary amount of common cultural sharing in lifestyles and preferences, especially among people below the age of 50.

In the USA, where there is now a much greater tolerance of religious freedom, partly due to the Constitutional emphasis on this aspect of civil liberties, partly perhaps due to the federal system, which allows for practices in some states which would not be per-mitted in others, and partly perhaps due to the strong Jewish lobby, the issue of religious beliefs and ritual practice has not had the same resonance as in Britain. Furthermore, the centrality of the history of the black slave population and the colonization of the native Americans looms large in a way incommensurate with anything in Britain, and understandably the debates are largely devoted to matters which arise in relation to redressing the injustices of the past. The new immigrant populations which have entered the USA recently have come from Hispanophone countries in the Caribbean and Mexico, and the cultural problems which they face owe more to language difficulties than to fundamentally different religious orientations. In Britain a new dimension to the question of inte-gration was introduced by the settlement of Muslim immigrants whose religious traditions were and are still not familiar to the host population.

Perhaps the most striking point to emerge from the comparison of the differences in emphasis which the two countries place on specific policies, however, lies in the observation that it is the very specific historical experience of the reception of different communities of immigrants, each with a unique demographic and cultural impact on the nation, which has determined both public perceptions and government policy. The USA has accommodated different waves of substantial numbers of migrants at different periods and the cumu-lative experience of assimilating and integrating those populations, not to mention dealing with much of the shameful legacy of the past, has led to a greater sensitivity to multicultural difference. In Britain, where in terms of the percentage of the population immigration has been limited and until the middle of the last century the presence of immigrants was not immediately visible, there has been perhaps an over-reliance on the process of natural assimilation which in the past seemed to have succeeded in turning immigrants into Englishmen within two or three generations.

Subsequently, the arrival first of a black population and then of a substantial Asian population from the Indian sub-continent and from East Africa has led to a re-evaluation of what had been a *laissez-faire* response to the presence of ethnic minorities. However, there is a strong body of informed opinion which argues that this re-evaluation has not gone far enough inasmuch as it fails to discriminate among the different immigrant populations and therefore fails to target disadvantaged groups appropriately since all are labelled as subject to the same forms of discrimination. Tariq Modood (1992), for example, has argued that to place British people of South Asian descent in a catch-all category of 'black' along with British people of Afro-Caribbean descent is to perpetuate this unhelpful blanket approach to social and economic issues which require a more sensitive handling.

Another way of perceiving the same problem is to observe how the lack of understanding of issues and of cultural context is revealed in differences with regard to questions of dual or hyphenated identity. In the USA, as we have seen, one refers happily to Chinese-Americans or Italian-Americans, acknowledging a primary identification with the nation but at the same time giving due weight to the significance of the culture of ethnic origin. In Britain the references are at best to British Asians or Afro-Caribbeans, with the implication being that these populations are still regarded as alien, with their primary allegiance being towards their country of origin, however remote the latter may now be for them. The linguistic difference may seem slight but reflects substantial differences in the reception of multicultural experience within the two nations. This is not to say, however, that one would necessarily endorse the notion of hyphenation, or 'hybridity' as it is called in some of the more abstruse discussions. As Caglar (1997: 172–7) points out in a very astute critique, this conceptualization of identity also presupposes an essentialization of culture in imagining the coming together of two in one.

Although both Britain and the USA share a common vocabulary of terms to discuss the experience of cultural difference within their populations, and although they share what might be regarded as a common position with respect to the philosophy of democratic liberalism and civil liberties, they have developed diverging approaches on the basis of liberal principles. Above all, they differ in the priorities which they assign to public policy as a consequence of their respective historical legacies. That there are yet further differences which we need to consider once we broaden our discussion to other countries is a fortiori true, and serves as a reminder to us, if we need it, that the talk of exporting the model from one country to another reflects simple-mindedness or arrogance or both.

Notes

1 But see McFarland (1991), who argues to the contrary that the attitudes adopted towards Indian and Chinese seafarers in Glasgow at that time developed into the later racism.

2 Bygott (1992: 56) makes the same point about early images, but goes on to say that these images have changed to more positive representations over the last few decades, though to my mind much more needs to change particularly in the representation of non-whites located in the setting of countries outside the North.

3 In this respect Alibhai-Brown (1999: 91–129) makes some useful suggestions about what might be done.

4 Kahn (1995: 116–22) is especially good on the contribution of European Jews to the discussion of American identity in the inter-war years and makes some interesting points about the origins of the multicultural debate in the USA as being established in this period. In addition, he points out that there were alliances between Jewish and black intellectuals, although he goes on to say that the Jewish lobby for a variety of reasons was more successful at that time (Khan 1995: 117). A further point which Kahn goes on to make in this context is the major role played at that time by American anthropology, led by Franz Boas, in elevating the status of minority communities by insisting on the intrinsic worth of their cultures.

5 The same argument is advanced, incidentally, to explain the insistence on, among other things, politically correct language, since it is argued that certain ways of referring and speaking to others, however much – and indeed precisely because – they are embedded in common usage, demean and humiliate others on account of their gender or ethnic origin.

6 One notes the increasing frequency with which these points are now being made not only in the USA but also in other parts of the world which have recently experienced dramatic change, for example, South Africa (see Jung and Seekings 1997).

7 This was the onus of Norman Tebbitt's infamous and fatuous reference to the cricket test when he maintained that a lack of loyalty to Britain could be perceived in the fact that British Asians and Afro-Caribbeans failed to support the English cricket team. Goodman, incidentally, in a recent comment on this issue (*Analysis* 1999), points out that, apart from anything else, allegiances of this kind change over generations and that generational depth must always be taken into account in understanding issues of loyalty to national symbols.

Conclusion

Among some academics the mention of 'cultural studies' sends a shudder down the spine, because of the way in which the rapid growth of the subject in university departments and academic circles in general conjures up the spectre of a monstrous colonization of disciplines each of which in the past had their own separate intellectual identity: literary studies, history, human geography, anthropology, politics, and even Marxism. Not only does this appear excessively predatory, it also seems intellectually regressive, conflating subjects which have only just taken on a separate existence in the curriculum.[1] Similarly, anyone reading the above account of multiculturalism might be forgiven for sharing the same misgivings after observing the tentacular growth of the term, which seems to bring within its range subjects as diverse as cuisine and clothing, ethnicity and nationalism, civil liberties and liberal democracy, education and religion, devolution and globalization. Is it really helpful to assemble all these topics together simply because issues of cultural diversity sometimes impinge upon them? How, one might wonder, has multiculturalism acquired such a wide and, in the eyes of some, such a debased currency?

As we have seen from our initial discussion of terms, part of the confusion has arisen from the different range of reference of the two terms 'multicultural' and 'multiculturalism', which though similar in appearance carry very different associations. 'Multicultural' points to the visible and universally accessible products of cultural diversity – food, clothes, music, theatre, and sometimes specialist occupations – and on the whole it has very positive resonance: we are all happy to live in multicultural societies which add to the variety and colour of lifestyles available to us, increasing the breadth of our choices as consumers. 'Multiculturalism', on the other hand, when it is not simply the noun from 'multicultural', directs our attention away from these purely visible aspects of diversity, to the deeper philosophical and political implications of the coexistence of different orientations to engagement with the world, and the way in which those differences jostle for recognition within national and global boundaries, sometimes in relative harmony with each other, sometimes in real conflict.

Another way of looking at the usage of the two terms is not to focus upon their semantic range, however, but to note how 'multicultural' can be linked to a perspective which has the individual at its centre (though we should note that in this respect the revitalized term 'cosmopolitan', as described by Hannerz (1990), is increasingly replacing it), whereas 'multiculturalism' compels us to think through the social and collective dimensions of diversity. This dichotomy has an especial relevance for discussions which circulate in Western liberal democracies where governance commences from the proposition that the aim of the state must be to limit the restrictions on individual action as little as possible, since the ultimate goal of human development must be the maximization of the potential of the individual. In this view the laws, structures and institutions of the state are, or should be, designed solely to enhance the possibility of individual freedom. Understandably, then, the additional dimension of individual choice which the word 'multicultural' suggests is welcomed. From other perspectives where the emphasis may be less on individual achievement as the ultimate goal, and more on the creation of collective well-being and the harmonious interaction of humans with the natural environment, the stress on individual satisfaction may not be such a useful yardstick for the evaluation of social and economic progress (Ostendorf 1998: 46–53).

Liberal society does recognize that checks must be put on individual liberty, in particular to safeguard the rights of those who may be endangered by the expression of that liberty. Even such sacrosanct institutions such as free speech or the freedom of the press are subject to laws of libel and defamation, and the interests of national security, and hence citizens of liberal democracies need constantly to be reminded that liberty is not licence. However, in Europe – with some exceptions such as Germany – and North America, there is a consensus concerning the centrality of the individual which has dominated discussions of civil liberty. It has only been very recently that, as a consequence of the dramatic effects of increased global mobility, liberal democracies have had to take account of a heterogeneity which challenges that fundamental focus on the individual and hence, allegedly, the basis of liberalism itself. It is here that 'multiculturalism' rather than 'multicultural' becomes significant, and this provides the justification for the extension of the discussion to include issues of identity, ethnicity, religion and nationalism.

Multiculturalism in this broader sense is a relatively new coinage but under different guises its implications have long been matters of direct concern to post-colonial nations where diversity and heterogeneity have been the rule rather than the exception. As the examples of the countries of Africa, the Indian sub-continent and Southeast Asia illustrate, arbitrarily created colonial political boundaries enclose within new and independent nations substantial populations which are ethnically distinct, or at least regard themselves as such, and their orientations, values and religious beliefs can often be at odds with each other. In these circumstances governments may frequently have less scope for the extension of freedoms to individuals because of fear of jeopardizing what is in many cases a fragile consensus.

Although we must be wary of the sometimes specious appeal to such reasoning in order to legitimate acts of state terrorism and violence, we should recognize that 'multiculturalism', when we apply the term to those countries, presents special problems of a kind different from those encountered in the countries of the North. Indeed, the fact that in the latter the new term 'multiculturalism' is preferred to the older terms such as 'pluralism' indicates an awareness of that difference. The social and political development which has occurred as a result of the incorporation of new immigrant populations, though engaging with the perennial issues of the compatibility of the rights and demands of people of different ethnic groups, religious orientations, linguistic backgrounds and sexual orientations,[2] owes its specific character to the unique set of historical and global circumstances which have arisen in the second half of the twentieth century. To be properly understood, that development needs always to be appropriately contextualized.

Contained within the new word 'multiculturalism', however, there lurks a potential danger in the naive understanding of culture which it assumes, and which it has been one of the principal aims of this book to dispel. The absurdity of much of the common misconception is demonstrated by the hand-wringing attempts to define a national culture, or even by those worthy discussions of what it means to be British or American or French and the attempt to institutionalize that national distinctiveness within educational curricula. Moves in this direction fail to understand that culture is a process of the constant adaptation of people to historical circumstances which requires them, as a condition of their own survival, to engage sympathetically with new ways of understanding the world and responding to it. Within that broad definition one can see immediately that there is considerable manoeuvre for individual sentiments and approaches to living in the world and that any attempt to define, or worse, to legislate for a culture is doomed to failure and is only perhaps worth contemplating in very specific historical circumstances as a temporary measure – for example, when working to achieve a national consensus in time of war, or in a post-colonial nation in order to create the ideological infrastructure for socio-economic development.

It is this failure to see culture (and for that matter ethnicity and religion) as a dynamic process of the constant evolution of forms, institutional, textual and ethical, and this persistence in thinking of it as an unchanging and finite set of essential characteristics, which lead to the designation of, for example, national cultures or religious cultures. One needs constantly to remind public opinion that reference to a Muslim culture is as limited and as useless for analytical purposes as Buddhist culture or Christian culture. The burning of a copy of *The Satanic Verses* in Bradford no more represents Muslim culture than the Vatican index of prohibited books or the Spanish Inquisition represents Christian culture. All are manifestations of an appeal being made to religion by a particular group of people at a specific time in history for a purpose which, to be properly understood, needs to be thoroughly examined in its context.

For as long as discussions on multiculturalism begin from the premise of culture as an assemblage of definitive characteristics, and governments continue to devise policy on that basis, either to accommodate what is thought of as the unchanging essence of alien cultural forms or to manufacture out of a set of cultural and historical ingredients what they seek to establish as a national culture, then the confusion surrounding the terminology is bound to persist. If we are usefully to retain the term 'multiculturalism' we must abandon those misleading associations of the word 'culture' with nations or ethnic groups or religious believers, and look much more closely at the changing ways in which the expression of identity responds to newly available local and global opportunities and how contained within those responses is an ongoing negotiation of collective and individual responsibilities which need to be configured less on a national than on a global or transnational scale.[3]

Whether we are trying to make sense of new post-colonial nations grappling with problems of ethnicity, religion and representation, or to pin down the malaise of post-modern capitalist societies seeking to balance the demands of their new citizens for justice, equity and the opportunity to be different, multiculturalism performs a useful service in recalling for us that there are several dimensions of experience at stake. Identity, and with it self-respect, is clearly one of them; a sense of belonging (to a community, to a religion, to a nation) is another; a sense of locality, of a commitment to a place (to somewhere recognized as home from the language one hears being spoken around one) is a third; and fourth is a sense of history arising out of a link to the past traced through kinship and family tradition. I have tried to touch on each of these aspects and illustrate their significance for various people, places and periods in history. Inevitably the descriptions have been sketchy and superficial, but I hope there has been enough of substance to confirm for the reader that multiculturalism, as a principle to be acted upon, requires from us all a receptivity to difference, an openness to change, a passion for equality, and an ability to recognize our familiar selves in the strangeness of others.

Notes

1 See Harvey (1996: 15), though she herself is favourably disposed towards cultural studies.
2 On sexual orientations, and on how such demands now borrow from an ethnic rights discourse, see Cohen (1997).
3 This issue of transnationalism is highly relevant to a discussion of multiculturalism but I do not have the space to pursue it here. Interested readers might like to turn to Soysal (1994).

References

Alibhai-Brown, Y. (1999) *True Colours: Attitudes to Multiculturalism and the Role of the Government*. London: Institute of Public Policy Research.

Alibhai-Brown, Y. (2000) *Who Do We Think We Are: Imagining the New Britain*. London: Allen Lane.

Alderman, G. (1995) 'The defence of *shechita*: Anglo-Jewry and the "humane conditions" regulations of 1990', *New Community*, 21(1): 79–93.

Analysis (1999) National portrait presented by Yasmin Alibhai-Brown, Radio 4, BBC, 2 December.

Anderson, M. (1990) 'The social implications of demographic change' in F. M. L. Thompson (ed.), *The Cambridge Social History of Britain 1750–1950*, Vol. 2. Cambridge: Cambridge University Press, pp. 1–70.

Appadurai, A. (ed.) (1986) *The Social Life of Things: Commodities in Cultural Perspective*. Cambridge: Cambridge University Press.

Apter, D. (1999) 'Les Violences de la mondialisation', *Le Monde*, 24 December, p. 16.

Asad, T. (1993) *Genealogies of Religion. Discipline and Reasons of Power in Christianity and Islam*. Baltimore, MD, and London: Johns Hopkins University Press.

Asad, T. (1999) 'Religion, nation-state, secularism' in P. van der Veer and H. Lehman (eds), *Nation and Religion. Perspectives on Europe and Asia*. Princeton, NJ: Princeton University Press, pp. 178–96.

Bak, H. (1993) 'The *Heath* is on: canon or kaleidoscope?' in H. Bak (ed.), *Multiculturalism and the Canon of American Literature*. Amsterdam: VU University Press, pp. 65–81.

Bateson, G. (1972) 'Culture contact and schismogenesis' in *Steps to an Ecology of Mind: Collected Essays*. St. Albans: Paladin, pp. 35–46. (First published in 1935.)

Baumann, G. (1992) 'Ritual implicates "Others": rereading Durkheim in a plural society' in D. de Coppet (ed.), *Understanding Rituals*. London and New York: Routledge, pp. 97–116.

Bin Zhao (1997) 'Consumerism, Confucianism, Communism: making sense of China today', *New Left Review*, 222: 43–59.

Bowie, F. (1993) 'Wales from within: conflicting interpretations of Welsh identity' in S. Macdonald (ed.), *Inside European Identities. Ethnography in Western Europe*. Providence, RI, and Oxford: Berg, pp. 167–93.

Brah, A. (1996) *Cartographies of Diaspora*. London and New York: Routledge.

Brown, D. (1971) *Bury My Heart at Wounded Knee*. London: Barrie and Jenkins.

Brown, J. M. (1985) *Modern India: The Origins of an Asian Democracy*. Oxford: Oxford University Press.

Bygott, D. (1992) *Black and British*. Oxford: Oxford University Press.

Caglar, A. S. (1997) 'Hyphenated identities and the limits of "Culture"' in T. Modood and P. Werbner (eds), *The Politics of Multiculturalism in the New Europe: Racism, Identity and Community*. London and New York: Zed, pp. 169–85.

Casanova, José (1994) *Public Religions in the Modern World*. Chicago: Chicago University Press.

Chicago Cultural Studies Group (1994) 'Critical multiculturalism' in D. T. Goldberg (ed.), *Multiculturalism: A Critical Reader*. Oxford: Blackwell, pp. 114–39.

Coedes, G. (1948) *Les États hindouisés d'Indochine et d'Indonésie*. Paris: E. de Boccard.

Cohen, C. J. (1997) 'Straight gay politics: the limits of an ethnic model of inclusion' in I. Shapiro and W. Kymlicka (eds), *Ethnicity and Group Rights: Nomos XXXIX*. New York: New York University Press, pp. 572–616.

Colley, L. (1992) *Britons: Forging the Nation 1707–1837*. New Haven, CT, and London: Yale University Press.

Crystal, D. (1999) 'The death of language', *Prospect*, 46: 56–9.

Daniels, Roger (1993) 'The Asian-American experience: the view from the 1990s' in H. Bak (ed.), *Multiculturalism and the Canon of American Literature*. Amsterdam: VU University Press, pp. 131–45.

Faisal Bodi, F. (1999) 'All religions must be protected', *The Guardian*, 26 November.

Ferenczi, T. (1995) 'Le Creuset français réussit encore a intégrer les nouvelles générations d'immigrés', *Le Monde*, 31 March: 8.

Fitzgerald, C. P. (1972) *The Southern Expansion of the Chinese People*. London: Barrie and Jenkins.

Forsythe, D. (1989) 'German identity and the problems of German history' in E. Tonkin, M. McDonald and M. Chapman (eds), *History and Ethnicity*. London: Routledge, pp. 137–56.

Furnivall, J. S. (1948) *Colonial Policy and Practice: A Comparative Study of Burma and Netherlands India*. Cambridge: Cambridge University Press.

Gellner, E. (1995) 'Sauce for the Liberal Goose', *Prospect*, 2: 56–61.

Gladney, D. (1991) *Muslim Chinese Ethnic Nationalism in the People's Republic*. Cambridge, MA, and London: Harvard University Press.

Gladney, D. (1997) 'Indigeneity and post-coloniality: the question of "minority" identity in China', *Cultural Survival Quarterly*, 21(3): 50–5.

Gladney, D. (1999) 'Representing nationality in China: refiguring majority/minority identities' in K. Yoshino (ed.), *Consuming Ethnicity and Nationalism: Asian Experiences*. Richmond, Surrey: Curzon, pp. 48–88.

Goldberg, D. T. (ed.) (1994) 'Introduction: Multicultural conditions' in D. T. Goldberg (ed.), *Multiculturalism: A Critical Reader*. Oxford: Blackwell, pp. 1–41.

Gray, J. (1999) *False Dawn: The Delusions of Global Capitalism*. London: Granta.

Grillo, R. D. (1998) *Pluralism and the Politics of Difference: State, Culture, and Ethnicity in Comparative Perspective*. Oxford: Clarendon Press.

Guha, R. (ed.) (1982) *Subaltern Studies I*. Delhi: Oxford University Press.

Gutmann, A. (1994) 'Introduction' in C. Taylor, *Multiculturalism: Examining the Politics of Recognition*. Princeton, NJ: Princeton University Press, pp. 3–24.

Hall, J. A. and Lindholm, C. (1999) *Is America Breaking Apart?* Princeton, NJ: Princeton University Press.

Hannerz, U. (1990) 'Cosmopolitans and locals in world culture' in M. Featherstone (ed.), *Global Culture: Nationalism, Globalization and Modernity*. London: Sage, pp. 237–51.

Hannerz, U. (1992) *Cultural Complexity: Studies in the Social Organization of Meaning*. New York: Columbia University Press.

Hargreaves, A. G. (1995) *Immigration, 'Race' and Ethnicity in Contemporary France*. London: Routledge.

Harvey, P. (1996) *Hybrids of Modernity: Anthropology, the Nation State and the Universal Exhibition*. London: Routledge.

Hicks, G. (1997) *Japan's Hidden Apartheid. The Korean Minority and the Japanese*. Aldershot: Ashgate.

Hill. J. D. (ed.) (1996) *History, Power, and Identity. Ethnogenesis in the Americas, 1492–1992*. Iowa City: University of Iowa Press.

Hiro, D. (1991) *Black British, White British* (revised and expanded edition). London: Paladin.

Holland, B. (1995) '"Kicking racism out of football": an assessment of racial harassment in and out of football grounds', *New Community*, 21(4): 567–86.

Hook, B. (ed.) (1991) *The Cambridge Encyclopedia of China* (New Edition). Cambridge: Cambridge University Press, pp. 75–84.

Hornung, A. (1998) 'The transatlantic ties of cultural pluralism – Germany and the United States: Horace Kallen and Daniel Cohn-Bendit' in

K. J. Milich and J. M. Peck (eds), *Multiculturalism in Transit: A German–American Exchange*. New York and Oxford: Berghahn, pp. 213–28.

Horrocks, D. and Kolinsky, E. (eds) (1996) *Turkish Culture in German Society Today*. Providence, RI, and Oxford: Berghahn.

Howell, D. W. and Baber, C. (1990) 'Wales' in F. M. L. Thompson (ed.), *The Cambridge Social History of Britain 1750–1950*, Vol. 1. Cambridge: Cambridge University Press, pp. 281–354.

Huntingdon, S. P. (1993) 'The clash of civilizations', *Foreign Affairs*, 72(3).

Jorno, K. S. (1989) Malaysia's New Economic Policy and national unity, *Third World Quarterly* (special issue, 'Ethnicity in world politics'), Vol. 11, No. 4, October, pp. 36–53.

Joppke, C. (1996) 'Multiculturalism and immigration: a comparison of the United States, Germany, and Great Britain', *Theory and Society*, 25(4): 449–500.

Jung, C. and Seekings, J. (1997) ' "That time was apartheid, now it's the new South Africa": discourses of race in Ruyterwacht, 1995' in I. Shapiro and W. Kymlicka (eds), *Ethnicity and Group Rights: Nomos XXXIX*. New York: New York University Press, pp. 504–39.

Kahn, J. S. (1995) *Culture, Multiculture, Postculture*. London: Sage.

Kane, J. (1997) 'From ethnic exclusion to ethnic diversity: the Australian path to multiculturalism' in I. Shapiro and W. Kymlicka (eds), *Ethnicity and Group Rights: Nomos XXXIX*. New York: New York University Press, pp. 540–71.

Kymlicka, W. (1995) *Multicultural Citizenship: A Liberal Theory of Minority Rights*. Oxford: Clarendon Press.

Lamey, A. (1999) 'Francophonia for ever: the contradiction in Charles Taylor's "politics of recognition" ', *Times Literary Supplement*, 23 July: 12–15.

Lim, M. H. (1985) 'Affirmative action, ethnicity and integration in the case of Malaysia', *Ethnic and Racial Studies*, 8(2): 250–76.

Lively, A. (1998) *Masks, Blackness, Race and the Imagination*. London: Chatto and Windus.

Macdonald, S. (1997) *Reimagining Culture: Histories, Identities and the Gaelic Renaissance*. Oxford and New York: Berg.

Mahathir bin Mohamad (1996) 'The Asian values debate'. Speech by the Prime Minister of Malaysia at the 29th International General Meeting of the Pacific Basin Economic Council, Washington, DC, 21 May.

Mann, M. (1999) 'The dark side of democracy: the modern tradition of ethnic and political cleansing', *New Left Review*, 235: 45.

McFarland, E. W. (1991) 'Clyde opinion on an old controversy: Indian and Chinese seafarers in Glasgow', *Ethnic and Racial Studies*, 16(4): 493–515.

Milich, K. J. and Peck, J. M. (eds) (1998) *Multiculturalism in Transit: A German–American Exchange*. New York and Oxford: Berghahn.

Miller, D. (ed.) (1993) *Unwrapping Christmas*. Oxford: Oxford University Press.

Modood, T. (1992) *Not Easy Being British*. London: Runnymede Trust.

Neary, I. (1997) 'Burakumin in contemporary Japan' in M. Weiner (ed.), *Japan's Minorities: the Illusion of Homogeneity*. London and New York: Routledge, pp. 50–78.

Nonini, D. M. (1997) 'Shifting identities, positioned imaginaries: transnational traversals and reversals by Malaysian Chinese' in A. Ong and D. M. Nonini (eds), *Ungrounded Empires. The Cultural Practice of Modern Chinese Transnationalism*. New York/London: Routledge, pp. 203–27.

Ostendorf, B. (1998) 'The politics of difference: theories and practice in a comparative U.S.–German perspective' in K. J. Milich and J. M. Peck (eds), *Multiculturalism in Transit: A German–American Exchange*. New York and Oxford: Berghahn, pp. 36–64.

Parekh, B. (1994) 'Superior people: the narrowness of liberalism from Mill to Rawls', *Times Literary Supplement*, 25 February: 11–13.

Parekh, B. (1995) 'The concept of national identity', *New Community*, 21(2): 255–68.

Parkin, R. (2000) 'Proving "Indigenity", exploiting modernity: modalities of identity construction in Middle India', *Anthropos*, 95: 49–63.

Parks, T. (1999) 'National character in Blair's new Britain', *The Independent*, 13 December: 7.

Peers, L. (1999) 'Revising the past: historic sites, the heritage elite, and challenges by native peoples in North America'. Paper presented at the ASA Annual Conference, Goldsmiths College, London, March.

Phillips, A. (1997) 'From inequality to difference: a severe case of displacement?', *New Left Review*, 224: 143–53.

Puhle, H.-J. (1998) 'Multiculturalism, nationalism, and the political consensus in the United States and in Germany' in K. J. Milich and J. M. Peck (eds), *Multiculturalism in Transit: A German–American Exchange*. New York and Oxford: Berghahn, pp. 255–68.

Raveau, F. H. M. (1968) 'Caste and race in the psychodynamics of acculturation' in A. de Reuk and J. Knight (eds), *Caste and Race. Comparative Approaches: A Ciba Foundation Blueprint*. London: J. and A. Churchill, pp. 266–75.

Redfield, R. (1954) *The Primitive World and Its Transformations*. Ithaca, NY: Cornell University Press.

Rex, J. (1996) *Ethnic Minorities in the Modern Nation State. Working Papers in the Theory of Multiculturalism and Political Integration*. London: Macmillan, in association with the Centre for Research in Ethnic Relations, University of Warwick.

Rushdie, S. (1991) *Imaginary Homelands*. London: Granta.

Samuel, R. (1994) *Theatres of Memory*. London and New York: Verso.

Schlesinger, A. M., Jr. (1998) *The Disuniting of America* (revised and enlarged edition). New York and London: W. W. Norton.

Seow, F. T. (1994) *To Catch a Tartar: A Dissident in Lee Kuan Yew's Prison*. New Haven: Yale University Center of Southeast Asian Studies.

Shapiro, I. and Kymlicka, W. (eds) (1997) *Ethnicity and Group Rights: Nomos XXXIX*. New York: New York University Press.

Silverman, M. (1992) *Deconstructing the Nation: Immigration, Racism and Citizenship in Modern France*. London: Routledge.

Sinha, S. (1967) 'Caste in India: its essential pattern of socio-cultural integration' in A. de Reuck and J. Knight (eds), *Caste and Race, Comparative Approaches*. London: J. & A. Churchill.

Soysal, Y. N. (1994) *Limits of Citizenship: Migrants and Postnational Membership in Europe*. London and Chicago: Chicago University Press.

Stenton, D. M. (1951) *English Society in the Early Middle Ages (1066–1307)*. Harmondsworth: Penguin.

Taylor, C. (1994) *Multiculturalism: Examining the Politics of Recognition*. With contributions from K. Anthony Appiah *et al.* Edited and introduced by Amy Gutmann. Princeton, NJ: Princeton University Press.

Thompson, F. M. L. (1990) 'Town and city' in F. M. L. Thompson (ed.), *The Cambridge Social History of Britain 1750–1950*. Cambridge: Cambridge University Press, pp. 1–86.

Trommler, F. (1998) 'Multiculturalism and the European connection: theme park or dual citizenship' in K. J. Milich and J. M. Peck (eds), *Multiculturalism in Transit: A German–American Exchange*. New York: Berghahn, pp. 167–82.

Turner, T. (1994) 'Anthropology and multiculturalism: what is anthropology that multiculturalists should be mindful of it?' in D. T. Goldberg (ed.), *Multiculturalism: A Critical Reader*. Oxford: Blackwell, pp. 406–25.

Vertovec, S. (in press) 'Fostering cosmopolitanism: a conceptual survey and a media experiment in Berlin', *Cultural Anthropology*.

Wagatsuma, H. (1968) 'The pariah caste in Japan: history and present self-image, (followed by) pariah castes compared, discussion' in A. de Reuk and J. Knight (eds), *Caste and Race*. London: J. & A. Churchill, pp. 118–65.

Watson, C. W. (1996a) 'The construction of the post-colonial subject in Malaysia' in S. Tønnesson and H. Antlöv (eds), *Asian Forms of the Nation*. Richmond, Surrey: Nordic Institute of Asian Studies/Curzon, pp. 297–322.

Watson, C. W. (1996b) 'Reconstructing Malay identity', *Anthropology Today*, 12(5): 10–14.

Wenden, C. Wihtol de (1991) 'Immigration policy and the issues of nationality', *Ethnic and Racial Studies*, 14(3): 319–32.

White, J. B. (1997) 'Turks in the new Germany', *American Anthropologist*, 99(4): 754–69.

Whitten, N. E. (1996) 'The Ecuadorian *levantamiento indigena* of 1990 and the epitomizing symbol of 1992: reflections on nationalism, ethnic-bloc formation, and racialist ideologies' in J. D. Hill (ed.), *History, Power and Identity*. Iowa City: Iowa University Press, pp. 193–217.

Wieviorka, M. (1998) 'Is multiculturalism the solution?', *Ethnic and Racial Studies*, 21(5): 881–910.

Williams, R. (1973) *The Country and the City*. London: Chatto and Windus.

Yamashita, S., Din, K. H. and Eades, J. S. (1997) *Tourism and Cultural Development in Asia and Oceania*. Bangi, Malaysia: Universiti Kebangsaan Malaysia Press.

Index

CULTURE
REINVENTING THE SOCIAL SCIENCES

Mark J. Smith

- How has the meaning of culture been reconsidered?
- What impact has this had on approaches to social enquiry?
- Should culture be seen as central to social science?

Over the past three decades there has been a transformation in the ways that social science has been conducted. In order to understand what is happening, we have to explore the implications of a rethinking of the meaning of culture, from a hierarchical system of classification to a contested space. This wide-ranging introduction to the concept of culture examines the ways in which we approach social enquiry, and argues that cultural theory can help to overcome problems in disciplinary and interdisciplinary analysis. Mark J. Smith explores how changes in the meaning of 'culture' have pinpointed key shifts in the way we research society, and draws on contemporary sociology, psychology, politics, geography and the study of crime to consider the ways in which cultural transformation has changed the landscape of social research. He concludes with a persuasive and focused discussion of the centrality of culture in post-disciplinary social science. This landmark text represents essential reading for students and researchers with an interest in the cultural dimension of social science.

Contents

160pp   0 335 20318 3 (Paperback)   0 335 20319 1 (Hardback)